More than the Game

Building Relationships for a Winning Culture

John Torrey

Wisdom Editions
Minneapolis

Wisdom Editions

Minneapolis

SECOND EDITION DECEMBER 2022
 Wisdom Editions is an imprint of Calumet Editions, 6800 France Avenue South, Suite 370, Edina, MN 55435.

10 9 8 7 6 5 4 3 2

ISBN: 978-1-960250-67-4

Cover design by Sue Stein
Book design by Gary Lindberg
Cover photo used by permission of Rhonda Rauch Photography

For Rachel

More than the Game

Building Relationships
for a Winning Culture

John Torrey

Chapter One

"You Might as Well Quit"

The cold October wind blasted through the multi-colored leaves still in the trees, pushing more to the ground as it made its way to Coach Warrington's windbreaker, causing him to shudder. He was a mountain of a man, six foot three and 215 pounds. He was now in his late thirties and still in elite shape, as if he could breeze through Hell Week with Navy SEAL hopefuls on Coronado Island any day, any time. The players referred to him as Coach War, partly because of his last name and physique and partly because his practice and game plans resembled an army's battle plan. As the varsity team ran the scripted offensive plays for one last time this season, Coach War stood aloof on the sideline, stooped, head down, with his ball cap covering most of his face. His chin rubbed against the inside of the zipper on the collar of his jacket; his hands were stuffed into oversized pockets of his sideline coat.

The season had not gone well. After winning their first two games, "L's" started to appear in the results column. The process of preparing from game to game each week did not change, but the energy and the team's will to win was gone. Coach War had lost the locker room. The running joke among teammates had become Edwin Starr's 1970 hit song. One person would ask, "War, huh, what is it good for?" And immediately another teammate would chime in, "Absolutely nothing, say it again!" No one had the balls to say this to Coach War's face, but he knew it was happening; Coach War *always* knew what his kids were up to. A shrill sound pierced the autumn air from a bullhorn in the end zone, signaling the end of the last practice.

Walking at a calculated pace gave Coach War time to retrieve the small notebook from the back pocket of his pants. Standing in front of a semi-circle of players, he flipped open the notebook cover. Keeping his head down, he began to speak.

"Tomorrow, you need to be at the high school by five p.m. You need to be dressed and ready to go by five thirty. Skill guys will take the field at 5:35, and linemen will come out at 5:50. Kickoff is at seven. Any questions?" Coach War paused briefly, lifting his head to look at the team before returning his notebook to his pocket. Eighty-three players gathered around him. Most of the players had their heads down, eyes fixed to the ground. His voice clenched as he prepared to deliver a necessary dose of reality directly to the underclassmen.

"As we look to next year, many of you are just not ready to play varsity. You're not big enough, strong enough, or talented enough. If you cannot *commit* to getting bigger, stronger, or faster, so our record can improve, then you might as well quit." He let his measured words hang in the air for a moment, then backed out of the semi-circle, beginning a lonely walk from the practice field end zone toward the field house locker room. The players rose to their feet, huddling together and placing their arms in the air for the traditional team break down.

"Victory on three," one senior yelled from the center. "One, two, three…"

"Victory!" cried the team.

And just like that, without ceremony or celebration, the season was, for all intents and purposes, over. Many of the players had been preparing for this moment, some even looking forward to it. They still had one final game, but the Titans had long been eliminated from postseason contention, and tomorrow's game would be the final straw in a long, disappointing season. For every one of the nineteen seniors, however, this was it—their last football practice ever, and there was not so much as a handshake or a thank you.

Chapter Two

Time for a Change

The Titans lost their final game, finishing the season two and seven. Players somberly lingered in the locker room, savoring one last moment with the seniors together as a team. They undressed at their lockers, stripping their helmets of team decals, numbers, and pride stickers. They were then expected to place team-issued gear into massive laundry piles as they made their way to the shower. Everything had its place. Heavy polyester game jerseys were heaved onto the floor, the sweat from the jerseys turning the cement a dark gray. Game pants and girdles comprised the next two piles, while insert pads were taped together in a set before being thrown into large cardboard boxes. Shoulder pads were to be stacked onto one of the two rolling metal carts in the adjoining equipment room, while helmets were placed on a large wooden shelf. These items may not have needed cleaning, but they did need to be reconditioned.

Opposite the showers was the coaches' office, which connected the varsity locker room to the field house and high school. Coach Warrington leaned forward in his favorite chair, watching film on his iPad. The assistant coaches sat on two adjacent couches looking on.

"See," Coach War blurted out to no one in particular. "Right there! If Jones makes this block, Remmy would have broken loose for a touchdown!"

The other coaches sat silently.

It was always the same postgame routine. The coaches would sit in the locker room until all of the players had left, second-guessing every critical decision made throughout the game. This usually meant criticizing the effort of their players or the officials. Coach War would watch that night's film and ask his staff what they felt their positions needed to work on throughout the next week in order to improve. The last game of the season was especially difficult because there was no "next week." The Titans would have to sit around for nine more months thinking about this loss. Coach War put his iPad down and ran his fingers through his hair.

A knock on the coaches' office door broke the silence, and in stepped Mr. Allen, the Titans' athletic director. Mr. Allen had always been a staunch supporter of Coach Warrington, believing he was the best man to lead Titan Football. Mr. Allen's son Jake had been an all-district quarterback for Coach War, leading the Titans to back-to-back playoff appearances. Jake viewed Coach War as a second dad. Eventually, however, their relationship had become strained by the pressure to win, and they had not talked since Jake's high school graduation. Seeing Mr. Allen caused Coach War's mind to drift. He suddenly remembered Jake and his pregame routine. Once dressed in full pads, he would sit on the bench next to his locker and tape his wrists. Using a black magic marker, Jake would write, "Phil 4:13" on the tape. Coach War thought about its meaning and longed for another playoff game. *I can do all things through Christ who strengthens me.*

He was interrupted by Mr. Allen's booming voice.

"Tough loss out there tonight, Coach," Mr. Allen began.

Tough season, Coach War thought, looking up from his iPad.

"I'll be honest, Coach," Mr. Allen continued. "The direction of this program needs to change, and I have some ideas that I think will make a difference. You're busy now, but come see me on Monday during your prep period. We can talk more then." Before Coach War could respond, the Titan AD had slipped out the door.

Chapter Three

The Meeting

The weekend passed, but Coach Warrington's worry did not. His mind jumped to conclusions. *What does Mr. Allen want? I know the season didn't go the way anyone had hoped, but I don't think it should cost me my job.* Coach War did his best to push these thoughts aside, keeping himself busy by watching film, doing team laundry, cleaning out the locker room, and even taking his kids to a movie. When his wife, Laura, asked him why he was so distant, Coach War replied that he was just trying to finish the season. Disgusted about how closed off her husband was on these matters, she dismissed her concern and knew not to probe any further.

Inevitably, Monday arrived. Coach Warrington's first and second period classes were a breeze. Mondays meant dodgeball. Many of his players were in these two periods, and the competition was fierce, especially when playing dodgeball. It was the perfect way to start the week, and usually Coach War looked forward to it. At 9:32 a.m., a beeping tone over the intercom sent kids scurrying throughout the building. Coach War monitored the locker room, ensuring that everyone was out of his area before walking down the hall to the high school office.

Coach War could see Mr. Allen standing in the office doorway as he walked down the long corridor. He noticed that Mr. Allen was wearing a striped navy-blue polo neatly tucked into pleated khakis. As

Coach War got closer, he could see the school logo, an ancient Greek helmet, embroidered on the shirt in white above the left breast. "Titan Athletics" was stitched in white script around the helmet. Reading glasses swung from side to side around Mr. Allen's neck on a lanyard as he extended his right hand and patted Coach War on the shoulder.

"Coach Warrington, thanks for coming. It's good to see you." Mr. Allen's gentle smile eased Coach War's worry. "C'mon in," he welcomed, escorting his friend down a narrow hallway to a corner office. Coach War sat in the nearest of two chairs across from the desk.

"Coach," Mr. Allen initiated, with just a hint of suspense in his voice. "You are a good leader and football coach, and I'm proud to also call you a friend. Your scheme is sound, and you've served our district well over the last twelve years. Plus," Mr. Allen continued, looking directly into Coach War's eyes, "you're a damn good PE teacher, which is why we hired you in the first place."

Coach War squirmed in his seat. *Why the hell am I here then?* he wondered, trying to keep his mind from racing to a million other things he should be doing.

"But," Mr. Allen said, "today's athlete isn't interested in a sound scheme. Heck, they can get *that* by 'asking Madden' on their video game."

Coach War allowed himself to laugh.

"My point is that if you want to win, I mean really win, then we need to improve your team's culture." Mr. Allen paused to let his message sink in. "Interested?"

Coach War reflected on what coaching the twenty-first century athlete was like. It was hard to get kids in the weight room consistently, especially in the summer and nearly impossible after the 4th of July—the most critical time of the year leading into the season. Teammates no longer talked to each other face-to-face, instead opting to communicate via Snapchat, Instagram, or Direct Message on Twitter. Communicating with a coach was worse. Rather than accept criticism and have an honest conversation about what they needed to do to improve in the future, kids would walk away in anger, quit, or even tell coaches to fuck off. And, worst of all, it was an age of sport-specialization where four-sport athletes were about as common as unicorns.

"So what do you have in mind?" Coach War inquired, always looking for an edge.

Mr. Allen leaned back in his chair, letting his eyes gaze up at the ceiling.

"I know a guy who can help you get the most out of your players. He's a former high school coach, and his area of expertise is sports psychology. I've already reached out to him, and he's willing to meet with you once a week for about an hour. He would become your mentor."

Coach War bit his lip, hiding his initial reaction. He was embarrassed that Mr. Allen would even *suggest* that he needed a mentor.

"Of course," Mr. Allen backpedaled, "it's your decision."

"I don't know, Bill. Let me think about it, and I'll let you know." Lifting his large frame out of the chair, Coach War walked out of Mr. Allen's office.

Standing from behind his mahogany desk, Mr. Allen hollered down the hallway, "He's got to know by Friday!"

Coach War did not even slow down. When he was out of sight, Mr. Allen slumped back into his leather wingback chair. He folded his hands on top of his head, wondering what Coach War would decide.

Chapter Four

Paralysis by Analysis

That night before dinner, Coach War rationalized why he *didn't* need a mentor, ranting to his wife.

"Next year we return fourteen offensive and defensive starters. With that kind of experience, culture won't matter. Plus, there will be more talent on the team. Remmy will be the fastest back in the district, as long as he wrestles and goes out for track this spring, and he'll be bigger and stronger. Wilson will easily be an all-district linebacker. We'll win more games based on these factors alone."

"Um-hum," Laura agreed, keeping her head low as she chopped the lettuce for the salad. The long knife punctuated the air with quick, staccato beats as she worked. Coach War wondered if she was even listening.

Still, the fact that the players buy-in and commitment had waned from game to game throughout this past season lingered in the back of Coach War's mind. The more the Titans lost, the harder it had become to manage his team. While he did not want to meet with a mentor each week, Coach War was intrigued by the idea of working on his team's culture. Still, his ego was unwilling to accept that he needed help. Coach Warrington's ambivalence was interrupted by his wife.

"What is it you always say to me?" she chimed in. "You know, that Eddie Roosevelt quote?" Her words hung trapped under the vaulted ceiling of the dining room as she placed the salad bowl in the middle of the table.

"*Teddy* Roosevelt," Coach War groaned. "*President Teddy* Roosevelt!" correcting her for at least the thousandth time. It was baffling to him that someone with a college degree did not know who President Roosevelt was.

"Yeah, that guy," she said dismissively. "You know, his quote. What is it again?"

Coach War swallowed a crouton as he recalled the correct wording.

"In any moment of decision, the best thing you can do is the right thing, the next best thing is the wrong thing, and the worst thing you can do is nothing." His wife's perspective fit his internal dilemma. He pushed the thought aside and enjoyed dinner with his family.

* * *

Mr. Allen's proposal came back to Coach War the next morning during his run. His personal mantra was "five at five"—a five mile run at five a.m. Every day, no exceptions. Not only did this keystone habit allow him to maintain optimal fitness, but it was usually the only personal time he got all day. After all, the only way to add more time in your day is to get up earlier. "I'll sleep when I'm dead," he would say. When his players would question him about why he always got up so early, Coach War would answer with a line from the United States Army. "Son," he would tease. "I do more before nine a.m. than most people do all day." His morning run was his dirty work. It helped him clear his head. Plus, Coach War relished knowing that he was willing to do things others weren't in order to accomplish things others couldn't.

Lacing up his running shoes in the predawn light of Friday morning, the thought of having a mentor was still gnawing at Coach War. While he originally dismissed the idea entirely earlier in the week, now he was more receptive to the possibilities it might bring. Step after step, his Nike Free shoes melodically pounded the pavement, the shoelaces gently slapping above his ankle. As he ran, Coach War thought about one of his first mentors—his college football coach, whose words haunted his mind between deep, cavernous breaths.

"You're either headed in this direction…" his coach would say in the huddle, extending his hand away from his body, his arm reaching upward toward the sky. "Or," he would add, pointing toward the ground, "you're headed in this direction." Coach made it clear that there was no other path for a team to be on... everything in between the two was a lie.

It didn't take a genius to diagnose the trend the Titans were on. Seven losses in a row was as sharp a nose dive as Coach War had ever experienced in twelve years of coaching. The first step to changing the direction of the program was to accept the help he had been offered.

When Coach War reached his driveway at the end of his run, he was soaked in sweat. His gray hoodie sported dark circles under each arm and around the neck. A plume of steam rose from his head before dissipating into the crisp early winter air, which pierced his lungs with each breath. He admired the beauty of the dark purple sky that was becoming lighter by the minute as his body returned to homeostasis. This was his favorite part of his day; a brief chance for clarity; a time for decision-making.

After a long moment, Coach War entered the garage code and slithered into his still dark house. He was tired of thinking about it. Paralysis by analysis. President Roosevelt's words turned over in his mind as he threw his workout clothes in the hamper and made his way to the shower. *In any moment of decision, the best thing you can do is the right thing, the next best thing is the wrong thing, and the worst thing you can do is nothing*. Tired of lying to himself, it was time for a change, and he was finally willing to act. The only thing left to do was to tell Mr. Allen.

Chapter Five

The First Week

Mitchell McClellen shuffled along the sidewalk, basking in the unseasonably warm air. With the temperature uncharacteristically climbing into the upper sixties, he slowed his gait even further to soak in a cloudless blue sky. Mitchell laughed to himself wondering why he bothered to bring his coat. The sun's glare spread across his glasses, making him squirm. He shifted his attention back to the path leading up to the Titans' athletic complex. Mitchell had retired from teaching several years ago but found an extra pep in his step as he approached the building. Each school he visited held a familiar charm, even if it was his first time.

Tuesdays had long been his favorite, dating back to the first time he had taught Mitch Albom's bestseller *Tuesdays with Morrie* in his sophomore Language Arts class. Reading one chapter at a time, Mitchell always left the kids wanting more. He reveled in the way they begged him to keep going each week. Remembering a line from the book, a smile crept across the creases of his face. *Mitch*, he thought to himself, *we're Tuesday people.*

Mr. Allen stood waiting for Mitchell in the atrium of the field house. Seeing Mitchell's whimsical grin made Mr. Allen long for the good old days when he was in high school playing quarterback and Mitchell McClellen was a tough, young go-getter who carried the title of Head Football Coach.

"I *knew* you'd be early," Mr. Allen greeted warmly. "Thanks for coming." Mitchell wrapped his former athlete in a big hug and a thousand years of memories came flooding back.

"C'mon," Mr. Allen said after a long moment, "we have work to do. I'll introduce you to Coach Warrington." The two old friends walked in step down the long corridor to the coaches' office, their comfortable silence filling the hallway.

Coach War was working feverishly to finalize the football team's offseason lifting and conditioning plan on his laptop just outside the coaches' office. Wasting time was not in his DNA, and he always tried to make the most out of every minute of his prep.

"Coach Warrington, I'd like to introduce you to a close friend of mine." Mr. Allen's words made him jump. He rushed to save his work, then looked up to see his boss standing in the doorway.

"This is Mitchell McClellen," Mr. Allen continued. "He will be working with you over the course of the next few weeks. I'll leave you two alone so you can get acquainted."

Coach War lumbered over to the coaches' office, pointing at two couches on opposite sides of a small table where he and Mitchell could sit. Mitchell lowered himself into the center section of the tattered brown leather couch closest to the door; Coach War took a seat on the opposite couch. He was shocked at how far he sank down at first, but then recovered by slightly leaning forward. After removing his coat and setting it on the seat next to him, Mitchell eased back and began the getting-to-know-you process.

"So, Coach, what's the good word?" Mitchell asked, crossing his left leg over his right. He folded his hands, pressing them neatly on top of his knee as he looked directly into Coach War's eyes.

What's the good word? Coach War thought, mocking Mitchell. *Who is this guy? Am I really supposed to meet with him every week? He's so damn old! Life has passed him by. What could he possibly teach me?*

"Tell me about yourself, Coach Warrington. Mr. Allen has mentioned great things."

Coach didn't know where to start, so he stammered through a short personal narrative beginning with playing safety at the University of

Okoboji where he was named the team's defensive captain his senior year. After his eligibility had expired, he sought a teaching position where he could coach. Now, for more than a decade, he had been here, working with Mr. Allen, teaching PE, and coaching the Titans on the gridiron.

"And your family?" Mitchell prompted, his eyes darting to the wedding ring on his left hand.

"My wife and I have three kids, an eight-year old daughter Maya, who is in third grade, a four-year old daughter Ella, and an infant son Max. Our house is crazy-busy. How about you?"

Mitchell drew in a long breath. "It's just my wife and me now. We live in Cedar Creek where I taught and coached for over forty years. We have two sons who are now adults with families of their own. Five grandkids keep us going, and I wish we could see them more."

Coach War was impressed that Mitchell would drive nearly an hour just to meet with him. He also appreciated Cedar Creek football's winning tradition and wondered if Mitchell had something to do with that. That thought piqued his interest. For the next hour, the two men talked superficially as they began to understand the basics of each other's life. When the clock neared ten thirty, Coach War got off the couch and moved toward the door. It was almost time for his next PE class.

"That must mean we are out of time," Mitchell noticed, accepting the social cue and rising from his seat. "Until next week, I guess." Mitchell lifted his coat off the couch cushion and reached into its pocket to retrieve a bright yellow sticky note. He handed it to Coach War.

"What's this?"

"I want you to do a little activity," Mitchell explained. "Think about this question, and we can talk about it next Tuesday." Coach War casually accepted the sticky note, affixing it to the nearest corner of his desk.

Chapter Six

The Pigeon and the Statue

Mitchell strolled down to Mr. Allen's office after Coach War headed to class. Waiting patiently in the lobby, Mitchell sat stationary in an office chair, observing. The two-tone blue Titan Pride decal jumped off the wall, its three-dimensional look reminding everyone of the school's brand messaging. The room buzzed with activity. Three secretaries sat in a row behind a chest-high counter answering the flurry of questions that flooded the phones. Jotting down brief notes on mini pads of paper, these women manned the front lines of the high school, neatly sorting each message into prioritized stacks. Even the Tasmanian devil would envy the pace they worked at, and their efficiency was almost German. This was a well-oiled machine.

Mitchell perked up when he saw three teenage boys being marched down to the office by a tall, thin man wearing gray pants, a white shirt, and a navy-blue paisley tie. *Must be the principal*, Mitchell thought. He watched the man in the power tie separate the three boys by taking one chair from each of the three adjacent walls and turning it backward. One by one the boys were sorted; the wall became their only vantage point. When the third boy was seated, the man moved to the center of the triangle, standing with his hands on his hips as his eyes scanned the room. His head pivoted back and forth.

Has to be some kind of investigation, Mitchell mused to himself. *I wonder what these guys did to get here*. He let his mind wander a bit, reverting back to his own teenage years. He recalled a short quote from *A Rumor of War* by Philip Caputo and repeated it in his head as he pondered the possibilities. "Before you leave here, sir," Caputo wrote while serving in Vietnam, "you're going to learn that one of the most brutal things in the world is your average nineteen-year-old American boy." Mitchell was busy contemplating the endless scenarios of mischief when one of the secretaries walked past the counter and offered to lead him down the office hallway.

Mitchell dismissed his daydream, rising out of the chair to follow the woman. Pictures of former Titan greats in their school uniforms lined both sides of the hallway. Each picture was framed in oak with a label uniformly placed in the lower left-hand corner of the frame. On it was the athlete's name, sport and position, year, and accolades accrued throughout that year's season. Mitchell's head toggled from side to side as they walked, and he noted how the styles had changed over the years. The most recent photos were closest to the secretaries. At first, athletes were decked out in Under Armour head to toe, but as the pair walked Mitchell began to notice Nike gear and oversized swoosh hoodies that read "JUST DO IT" in block letters. And when he saw football players wearing mesh jersey half-shirts, he began to smile. Still, Mitchell's favorites were the frames closest to Mr. Allen's office. Dark gyms, Daisy Duke shorts, knee-high tube socks, and afros dominated pictures of athletes from the seventies and eighties. Some of these photos were color, but the earliest had been taken in black and white.

Mitchell could see that Mr. Allen was on the phone when he reached his office doorway. Holding the phone receiver in his right hand, Mr. Allen gestured for Mitchell to come in and sit down with his left. When he did, the secretary walked back to her desk.

"I've got to go," Mr. Allen said, wrapping up his business, "but I'll see you next week at the district ADs' meeting." He paused. "OK, very well. Buh-bye." Mr. Allen exhaled, frantically scratching something on the yellow legal pad in the middle of his desk.

Whatever that is must be important, Mitchell thought as he watched Mr. Allen stab three exclamation points onto the end of a sentence. The phone receiver clicked as Mr. Allen returned it to its base. He leaned back in his chair, giving his full attention to Mitchell.

"So, how'd it go?"

Mitchell raised his hand to eye level, shaking it back and forth.

"Well, did he seem receptive to you meeting with him?"

"I think so, but you know the first phase in the Process of the 'Ship. Relationships take time. Remember, it takes no fewer than seven days, but no more than seven years to build trust."

Mr. Allen nodded, thinking he must have heard Mitchell say that phrase one hundred times in his life.

"Well, thank you for taking time to come and meet with him. I'm hopeful that Coach Warrington will reap big rewards in the harvest of your meetings. See you next Tuesday?"

Mitchell nodded and paused, looking into Mr. Allen's icy-blue eyes.

"Are you OK?"

"It's a whirlwind in here," Mr. Allen generalized. "There's never enough time in the day to put out all the fires. At least there's never a dull moment."

"No," Mitchell agreed. "Not in leadership. But you're able to handle your responsibilities and duties? Your life's in balance?"

"Some days you're the pigeon. Some days you're the statue," Mr. Allen quipped as he read the note on top of a sizable stack of papers. He grimaced as he felt the heat of his next fire. "Some sophomore boys just shit, and I've got to get it cleaned up."

"Guess today you're the statue," Mitchell joked. They both laughed as Mr. Allen stood and walked out from behind his desk to shake Mitchell's hand. He patted him on the back once more before the old friends walked arm in arm back to the main office's doors.

Chapter Seven

Beginning the Journey Inside

The small note rested untouched on the corner of Coach War's desk throughout the entire next week. *Damn it*, he complained to himself on Tuesday morning, the fluorescent sticky note chiming like an incessant alarm clock. *Mitchell will be here today*. He briefly considered just ignoring the assignment, faking his way through today's mentoring session. *After all*, Coach War justified, *I've always been good at thinking on the fly*. Though it was tempting, Coach War quickly dismissed this act of deception. He had given Mr. Allen his word, committing to the weekly meetings with Mitchell. One thing he could not stand was a cheater, and his conscience would not let him cut corners on his first assignment. Lifting the sticky note off his desk, he folded it in his hands and tucked it into the front left pocket of his coaching pants.

After taking attendance in his first period class, Coach War started the students on the day's activity by dividing them into six groups to play knockout. Standing in the small circle at midcourt in the gym, he unfolded the note. He was baffled. *This looks as if it was written by a toddler.* Scratched out in shaky lines was one, four-word question, which he read to himself: "Why do I coach?"

Coach War nearly laughed out loud. *That's it?* he thought, rubbing the paper between his index finger and thumb. *That question is supposed to take me an entire week to answer?* His lips turned into a grin at the sight of a student completely air-balling his free throw attempt. Coach War crushed the note in the palm of his right hand.

"Easy," he said to himself, narrowing his eyes. "Win."

* * *

Mitchell arrived later that morning in his usual cheery mood. After a moment of small talk in the coaches' office, idol banter began with, "So, how was your week?" and was followed by a scripted answer like, "Good, yours?" Coach War cut to the chase.

"So, you want to know why I coach, huh?"

Mitchell was caught off-guard by Coach War's pointedness.

"Why, yes, I would like to know your purpose."

Leaning back into the couch, Coach War stated, "Because I like to win." He crossed his feet, propping them up on the coffee table that separated the two couches.

"I see," Mitchell responded. "All the time?"

"All the time. I don't care if I'm coaching football, playing cards or yard games, setting my lineup for fantasy football, or running a dead sprint. I'm going to win." Coach War smirked, thinking about one of the most famous lines in his favorite movie *Talladega Nights*: "If you're not first, you're last." Coach War *lived* to win.

"And what happens if you don't?"

"What do you mean?"

"I mean no one can win all the time. Think about a time this season when your team didn't win. How did you feel?"

Coach War internalized Mitchell's question for a long moment. *Should I disclose how no one in my family wants to be around me after a loss on Friday night? Or how after the worst losses, the ones by a large or slim margin, I drink myself into a stupor to temporarily forget the game and numb the pain?* Coach War sat silently as the gravity of Mitchell's probing sank in, his eyes revealing the hurt of his transactional coaching style. Mitchell could see the inside-out process begin to take hold.

"Winning cannot be your purpose, Coach. Is it nice to win? Of course. But you cannot control winning. What you can control is the belief that what you are doing matters and that you are making a difference. Your actions need to be so clear that other people can see that you are making a difference too. Everything you say and everything you do should let people know your purpose as a coach. You are the builder of your program." Mitchell paused. "You see, average leaders give people things to work *on*. Transactions and rewards. If you do 'X,' you will get 'Y.'"

Coach War's mind jumped to the Titan off-season lifting plan he was preparing. Written in bold beneath his workout schedule was the following announcement: "Players who complete 80 percent of these workouts will receive a Titan Strength shirt." Following that was an image of the dark-blue, Nike Dri-FIT shirt. His eyes glanced from side to side, and he hoped the expression on his face did not give him away.

"Don't worry, Coach," Mitchell reassured. "You are not the only leader who wants to win at all costs. But, in my opinion, the best leaders also inspire others. They give people something to work *toward*. These are the leaders who change the world. Consider Henry Ford. When Ford was asked what it was like to create the Model T, he responded, 'If I had asked people what they wanted, they would have said faster horses.' Ford was changing the world behind a cause. He wanted to shift people's lives through innovation. If you want to win, become an innovator. Do things that others are not."

Coach War slumped in the chair, stunned. His entire coaching career seemed empty and meaningless. He knew that Mitchell was right. The wins were fleeting, and it was because he was never satisfied. He mandated his players to practice the Twenty-Four-Hour Rule. "Enjoy this one for twenty-four hours," he would say in the locker room amid the hoopla after a win. "But then it's back to work." There was always another game to prepare for. Losses were worse—much worse. Even after a decade of coaching, Coach War could recall nearly every final score in games where the Titans came up short. These numbers haunted him like ghosts.

"OK," Coach War agreed, ready to flip the script. "Let me ask you, what's *your* purpose, Mitchell?"

"My purpose is to help others sharpen their axe."

"Huh? What does that mean?"

"A long time ago," Mitchell began, "a lumberjack asked a timber merchant for a job. The pay was really good, the working conditions were favorable, and the lumberjack was motivated to do his best. The merchant supplied the lumberjack with the best axe money could buy and showed him where he could work."

Coach War thought about signing his first contract with the Titans. He was an optimist, fresh out of college, just happy to have a job that could provide more than pocket cash and an opportunity to do what he loved. He related to the lumberjack. *The work is hard,* Coach War thought, *but that is why it is important.*

"As dusk descended," Mitchell resumed, "the lumberjack proudly showed the merchant the pile of trees that he had felled throughout the day. This wood was ready to be carted to town to sell. The merchant was pleased, counting twenty-three cords. The lumberjack was satisfied with his work and felt proud of the effort he gave. He returned to the forest the next day even more motivated. But, by the end of the second day, there were only nineteen trees cut and placed in a pile. More strain and effort only yielded sixteen trees after the third day. In fact, every day that he worked, the lumberjack produced fewer and fewer trees."

Coach War sat forward, actively listening to Mitchell tell the story. He remembered going winless in his first season with the Titans and related to the disappointment the lumberjack was experiencing. "What happened next?"

"Well, the lumberjack asked himself all kinds of questions about why his production was declining at such an alarming rate. He decided to go to work earlier so he could spend more hours in the forest, but his numbers continued to fall. He tried using another swing style to chop at the trees, but that didn't work either. He even slept more at night to optimize his body's rest time to regain strength. Still, the number of trees he cut down each day declined. Exhausted and embarrassed, the only thing left to do was approach the merchant and apologize for his dwindling performance."

Coach War knew the feeling. Inside all driven people is the constant nag that they should be doing more.

"So how did the merchant respond?" Coach War inquired.

"Well, the merchant listened patiently to the lumberjack. He knew the lumberjack was committed to his job and gave great effort every day. So after the lumberjack had explained, the merchant asked, 'When was the last time you sharpened your axe?' The lumberjack was stunned. 'Sharpen my axe?' he questioned. 'When do I have time to do that! Every second of every day is spent in the forest cutting down trees.'"

Mitchell paused. He watched Coach War absorb the parable. "You see, Coach, our lives are like the lumberjack's. Sometimes we are so focused on what we are doing… running around, trying to meet deadlines… that we don't take time to sharpen our axe. Then, when our performance drops, so does our motivation and personal happiness."

Coach War nodded.

"Periodically, our axe needs to be sharpened. We need to make time for ourselves… to reflect, to learn new skills, to collaborate and connect with others, to relax and unplug. If we don't set aside time to do this, our lives, like the lumberjack's axe, become dull, and we lose our significance."

A loud bell pierced the stillness of the coaches' office, snapping Coach War out of his trance. He didn't want to go to his next class. He wanted to stay with Mitchell for another hour and talk more.

"I guess that's all for today," Mitchell concluded, extending his hand. "See you next Tuesday?"

Chapter Eight

Bachelor's, Master's, and PhD

That night Coach War lay awake in bed, surrounded by silence. His mind was restless, and it would not allow him to fall asleep. Staring into the darkness of his master bedroom, he pictured himself as the lumberjack. He closed his eyes to feel his hands wrap around the leather handle of the heavy axe. His shoulders tensed as he lifted the ax-head off the ground. The lumberjack's initial swing was wild, knocking him off balance, almost to the ground. Coach War had not anticipated the power of gravity as he hurled the blade toward the first tree.

The lumberjack stepped back from the tree to regroup before swinging again. This time the ax-head collided with the bark, scattering a thousand tiny splinters into the air. Over and over the lumberjack toiled against his opponent, who stood tall in front of him, easily four or five times his size. He had become winded after only a few blows. The lumberjack paused to catch his breath, giving him time to admire the sounds of the forest. Coach War could hear his labored breathing and feel tiny beads of sweat dripping off his forehead, stinging his eyes. After a few blows, he was able to work the cut, the axe grooving into rings of unexposed strength. The lumberjack hypnotized Coach War.

Mrs. Warrington's voice brought Coach War back to reality.

"What's wrong?" she questioned. Over a decade of marriage had given Laura spidey-senses that tingled whenever her husband was on edge.

"Huh? Nothing," Coach War grumbled, caught off-guard. He turned onto his side, rolling closer to the edge of the bed. He closed his eyes, allowing his mind to wander. He conjured a young version of himself on campus at the University of Okoboji.

Vinny Warrington was a "super senior," a fifth-year student capitalizing on one final semester of intercollegiate athletics eligibility. One evening in the fall of his second senior year, he returned to his dorm room after eating dinner in the cafeteria. Coach War recalled how the bulky room key in his left hand would get stuck in the lock. Holding an ice cream cone in his right hand and his keys in the left, he would awkwardly shift his body to spring open the sticky lock. On that particular night, Vinny had heard his dorm room phone ring through the heavy wooden door. He had panicked, dropping his ice cream cone on the hallway floor as he opened the door and jolted toward the phone.

"Hello?" he answered on the seventh ring, out of breath. He was *just* in time to hear Mr. Allen's voice.

Vinny had met Mr. Allen the day before when he interviewed for the Titans' PE opening beginning in January. That night, Mr. Allen was calling to offer him the job.

"Thank you," Vinny had responded, accepting the offer on the spot. He was so excited to get an offer that he didn't even ask about the details. Vinny set the cordless receiver back in its base, then let out a voracious "YES!" that echoed throughout the dorm. In less than two months, Vincent Warrington would leave the University of Okoboji as a three-year varsity letterman with a diploma, the first Warrington to graduate from college. And now he had secured his first job.

To Vinny, the bachelor's degree in secondary education was really a master's and PhD all rolled into one. Originally recruited to play quarterback, Vinny Warrington had found himself eighth on the depth chart at his first pre-season camp. As a redshirt freshman, it was his job to lead the scout team offense, comprised of other newbies, against the varsity starting defense every day at practice. Blitzing linebackers smelled blood in the water and knocked him around so much that at the end of the season Vinny's coach awarded him an honorary master's degree in getting back up. And, when spring ball began in March, Vinny Warrington had outgrown his scout team role, joining the defense where he would lead the secondary as a free safety. Still, he never forgot about his honorary master's degree. Vinny taped it to the inside of his locker, where it would hang until he received his official diploma.

Vinny's time at Okoboji was quickly drawing to a close. While there was still a little football left to be played, and four classes to pass, Vinny was excited to get to work. In addition to his master's degree, Vinny also held a PhD. He was "Poor, Hungry, and Driven," like the lumberjack in Mitchell's story. As the son of a blue-collar worker, the only way Vinny could afford college was through student loans, which he had maxed out. He did not have much… *yet*. But his father had taught him the value of a dollar, and he knew the statistical wage difference that came with a college degree compared to those with just *some* college. Most importantly, Vinny had the heart of a prize fighter; he was a scrappy athlete who possessed a strong desire to succeed. Now that he had a job, he could begin to change the world by making a difference in young people's lives as a teacher and coach.

Coach War's mind eased, brushing away the memory of Okoboji and the thought of the lumberjack as he finally drifted off to sleep. Over the next several weeks, Coach War's relationship with Mitchell grew. Even Coach War was surprised at how quickly he was able to trust Mitchell and rely on his sound advice. He even looked forward to their Tuesday meetings and hoped Mitchell did as well. As late fall faded into winter, and winter melted into spring, Coach War began to renew his energy and live a purpose-driven life. His axe was beginning to sharpen. He had never realized how dull it had become.

Chapter Nine

Summertime

The cherry blossoms lining the median of Titan Drive were in full bloom as graduation weekend arrived. The pink buds fell beautifully against the light-blue backdrop, and the sun was shining high in a cloudless sky. The green grass was freshly mowed, butting against the dark-blue brick high school, and the cherry blossoms' sweet perfume wafted through the air. Coach War was contractually obligated to attend and supervise graduation, another tedious task amid his list of professional duties. Mitchell surprised Coach War, who was in the coaches' office zipping up his faculty robe before heading to the gym.

"Mitchell!"

"Coach," Mitchell said with a smile, "it's good to see you."

"You too," Coach War fired back, and he meant it.

"I know it's summer, and we won't be meeting regularly, but I think we've made progress each week, and I would like to keep our momentum going. Are you willing to meet from time to time throughout summer break now that you will have more free time?"

Coach War thought to himself. *Free time*? *What free time?* With three young kids, summer meant Daddy Daycare at home and weight room supervision at school. While educators need summer to slow down, refuel, and recharge, Coach War's summer allowed him to substitute family time for contract time. Just like coaches who transition from sport to sport as the seasons rotate throughout a calendar year, summer was merely a transition into a different leadership role for Coach War. Still, he agreed with Mitchell and wanted to keep sharpening his axe.

"I'm a morning person," Mitchell continued. "Would you be willing to meet for coffee and a roll every so often? It wouldn't have to be each week, but maybe more frequently than once a month?"

Most teachers would grimace at the prospect of getting up early during summer, electing to sleep in instead, but that's not how Coach War was wired. He thought about his summer morning routine. Coach War would "sleep in" each day, pushing his run back to six a.m., a little reprieve from his "five at five" grind. If Mitchell was willing to meet at seven a.m., Coach War could get his run in *and* be back to his house in time to watch the kids so his wife could get to work on time. Coach War seized the opportunity.

"Sure, can we meet sometime this week? My wife has to be to work by nine o'clock, but we could meet at seven, if that's not too early for you—after all, *you're* the one driving."

"Perfect," Mitchell replied. "My wife is a morning person too. I can probably coax her into coming along most weeks by offering to buy her a cappuccino and a scone."

"Great! I know the perfect place," Coach War offered. "Are you familiar with ChapaChino on Main Street?"

"I'm sure I'll find it," Mitchell nodded.

ChapaChino would always hold a special place in Coach War's heart. A few years ago, Julio Chapa and Cesar Chino had been elite play-side wide receivers for the Titans, both earning all-district honors. While they each had a few offers to play small college ball, they decided to become entrepreneurs, opening a small gourmet coffee shop and staying close to their families. The idea of running a coffee shop was probably Coach War's. Every day at practice during static stretching, an assistant coach would go down the clipboard, taking attendance. Chapa and Chino's names were back-to-back on his roster, which was in alphabetical order. These two names rolled off Coach War's tongue, and he joked how you "couldn't have one without the other." Then one day, with Mr. Allen on the sideline observing, Coach War made a casual comment about how the two should open a coffee shop, which could be called ChapaChino. Everyone laughed in agreement. And so, ChapaChino was born. Meeting Mitchell there for coffee seemed fitting, since even *that* had started on the Titan football field.

"Tuesday?" Coach War questioned, rhetorically, shooting Mitchell a sly glance.

"I was hoping you'd say that," Mitchell confirmed. He shared Mitch Albom's words with Coach War before walking to the gym to take his seat for the ceremony. "We are Tuesday people."

Chapter Ten

"The Process of the 'Ship"

Mitchell drove home after graduation to prepare for his meeting with Coach War later that week. He brainstormed various ways that would help make their time productive throughout the summer. Possible ideas flashed in his mind as quickly as the dashed yellow lines that were painted on the highway. By the time he pulled his small SUV into the two-car garage attached to his house, Mitchell had not fully decided on the pair's next steps. He hung his keys on the hook and entered his house through the kitchen.

"Honey, I'm home!" he bellowed down the hallway, his tone warm and gleeful. While this saying is a cliché, it had been their routine for nearly forty-five years now. His wife was baking, and the aroma of warm cookies was too tempting. Mitchell's mouth watered; the entire house smelled like gooey chocolate. He bypassed his wife, going straight for a batch of cookies that looked to be fresh from the oven. He lifted one off the counter.

"Ouch!" he screamed, fumbling the cookie.

"Serves… you… right," she scolded. "You can wait until they cool. Besides, they aren't for you anyway."

"I'll be in my study if you need me," he called down the hall. He quickly reappeared around the kitchen corner. By this time his tie had been loosened. "And let me know when those cookies are cool!"

While some men have a man cave or garage for solitude, Mitchell had a study; it was his sanctuary. A small bedroom had been converted into a personal office after his oldest son had gone to college. Mitchell would have preferred it be bigger, a loft perhaps, but it was nice to have his own quiet space to think and reflect. The focal point of the room was a large picture window in the middle of the wall that faced north. Through the window was an expansive wetland that held a small pond and timber. The view had always been Mitchell's favorite feature of the house. Beneath the window was a large oak desk, Mitchell's blank canvas for whatever he wanted to read or write. An oversized black leather office chair on wheels allowed Mitchell to relax there comfortably for hours. The opposing walls of the window were lined with bookshelves that ran from floor to ceiling. Game balls and pictures from his coaching days interrupted long lines of his favorite books. Every inch was accounted for, and there was no extra space. One of Mitchell's favorite hobbies was to meticulously shuffle his memorabilia around. This was his domain, and while his wife did not understand that she did respect it.

Standing in the dimming light, Mitchell stared at a section of the bookshelf reserved for his coaching notes. Every season at Cedar Creek, he had issued a team binder to each of his players and assistant coaches. Inside the binders was a smattering of papers that usually included that year's team handbook, game plans, scouting reports, statistics and results, and weekly themes. Mitchell's binders were his prized possession, each crammed with short stories, newspaper articles, motivational quotes, and pictures—anything he had used to fuel his team's performance and his players' personal development. While the content changed from year to year, the binder was always called "The Winner's Manual."

Mitchell pulled a few at a time off the shelf, combing through each thoroughly, his eyes scanning the pages like a pirate searching the high seas for a ship to rob. As he finished each manual, he set it neatly in a stack on the corner of his desk so that it could be returned to its rightful place later. Mitchell searched through binder after binder.

C'mon, c'mon, he thought. *Where are you?* By the eighth binder, he had become frantic. Then he saw it—big, bold letters jumped off the page. Staring at them, he breathed a sigh of relief. In cursive was an early draft of his own coaching philosophy. Mitchell read the note aloud. "The Process of the 'Ship."

Chapter Eleven

The First Phase: Relationships

ChapaChino bustled as the workers prepared for and served the early morning rush. Machines hissed and steamed; workers hurriedly attended to each customer's morning needs. Trays of bagels, scones, and pastries were carted out and stacked in long lines under the glass countertop. In a far corner of the shop, one employee was drawing colorful caricatures of that day's specials on a chalkboard. Mitchell was reading the paper in a small corner booth when Coach War walked in wearing a faded T-shirt and sweatpants. Coach War gingerly shuffled through the counter line, sore but satisfied after his morning run. He ordered a tall coffee and a jelly-filled doughnut and paid before joining Mitchell in the booth.

"I was hoping I would beat you here so I could buy your coffee," Coach War said, setting his cardboard to-go cup on the booth top.

"Ah, you've got to get up earlier, then," Mitchell said smiling. "I believe that if you are on time, then you're late."

The two friends sat in a comfortable silence as they sipped their beverages. Eventually, Mitchell spoke up.

"Coach, I'm so proud of you. You successfully finished another year and are better equipped with a sharper axe to cut down more trees."

Coach War recognized his personal progress and agreed with Mitchell.

"But," Mitchell resumed, "now your *team* needs our attention. I've spent most of the last year getting to know you and helping you discover your purpose. While that needs to be done all the time, because you are always changing and growing, we need to move past you and focus on your team's culture."

Coach War nodded in agreement. *Finally*, he thought. *Now we're getting somewhere.*

"I want you to answer the following question," Mitchell continued. "How do you define success? And remember, your answer *cannot* be winning."

Coach War looked away. Mitchell would wait. One of his greatest strengths was wait time, a skill he had perfected throughout his career as a classroom teacher. The question was largely rhetorical; Mitchell knew that Coach War would be unable to answer it, but was surprised to hear Coach War's response.

"If wins do not count," Coach War explained, "then I guess I really don't know what success is."

Mitchell recognized and appreciated Coach War's honesty. That was a sign of growth.

"When I was coaching," Mitchell explained, "I had a three-phase blueprint to evaluate my team's success. That blueprint was designed to help my athletes grow and embrace the journey in front of them. I called it 'The Process of the 'Ship,' and I want to share the first phase of this process with you now."

Coach War leaned in, resting his elbows on the edge of the table. He folded his hands and fixed his eyes on Mitchell as waiters scurried past their booth.

"The first phase is relationships." Mitchell paused, taking a long pull from his coffee.

"Relationships?" asked Coach War, perplexed as to why this topic warranted an entire phase in Mitchell's blueprint.

"Coach, relationships are essential. You cannot pursue victory with honor *until* you have captured the hearts of your athletes. And, if you don't purposefully work to build relationships with your athletes, the games are meaningless, even if you do win."

Mitchell took another sip of his drink before continuing.

"But, if you can capture the hearts of young kids, you will provide them with a treasure house of memories that will last throughout their lifetime... well beyond your own. You will be able to leave a significant legacy. Tell me, what do you do to build and cultivate meaningful relationships within your program?"

Leaning away from the booth, Coach War scratched his head. He was at a total loss. He could not think of one way that he helped young men connect with others. Of course, Mitchell was expecting this, and his follow-up reflection cut deeper.

"Now think about all the players that you *could* have had a greater impact on."

Coach War's mind raced. The first thing he thought of was the large brass bell that he affixed to a wooden post on the perimeter of the practice field, modeled after the Navy SEALs. The Titans' rule was that a player could quit anytime practice got too hard without saying anything. All they had to do was ring the bell on the way down to the field house.

"Ring the bell," coaches would yell, "and you will never have to run another Titan 300!" The most common form of punishment, a Titan 300 was a sprint around the perimeter of the practice field, roughly the equivalent of 300 yards. Jump offsides? Run a Titan 300. Late to practice? Run a Titan 300. Talk back to a coach? Run a Titan 300. Players were constantly running during practice, but all of that could be stopped by ringing the bell.

"Ring the bell, and you'll never have to compete in another Oklahoma drill!"

"Ring the bell, and you won't get your ass pounded on the scout team anymore."

Coach War realized that this tactic was largely fear-based, but the bell took care of problems so he didn't have to.

Coach War's thoughts turned like a rolodex as ghosts from past seasons emerged to haunt him. One by one, a single-file line of kids formed in his mind. These were the kids who had quit because he never took the time to get to know them on a personal level. Every year kids quit, giving Coach War excuses like "I just don't have fun," or "football is boring." Until now, he never considered that there was anything wrong with this. After all, he was the coach. He expected his players to do things *his* way. Besides, wasn't it better if a kid quit because they couldn't handle a hard practice than if they quit on the goal line during a crucial moment of a close game?

Mitchell waited, eyeing Coach War as he saw the rolodex keep turning. At the end of the wheel, stashed deep in Coach War's subconscious, were the somber faces of first Brett Baxter, then Lance Munson, two former Titans on different teams who died by suicide after each was bullied in the locker room and throughout school. Brett and Lance had each joined the football team hoping to connect with others, but instead quit in the middle of their respective seasons. After Lance's death, school administration, including Mr. Allen, ordered that a full investigation be conducted to determine if hazing existed within Coach War's program. Former and current players, coaches, parents, and community members were called in and formally deposed. Ultimately a judge ruled that there was no hazing in Coach War's program and that he was not responsible for either player's death, but the investigation stung.

Mitchell eased Coach War's internal discomfort. "For our next meeting," Mitchell challenged, "I want you to brainstorm specific ways you can foster relationships within your program next season. Write down several possibilities you would be willing to explore, then circle your top three. Get creative. I'm excited to see what you will come up with."

Silently, Coach War nodded in acceptance. He shook Mitchell's hand and left the shop.

Chapter Twelve

War Report

Two weeks passed before Coach War saw Mitchell again. They met in the same booth at the same time at ChapaChino. Coach War was apprehensive about their meeting. He really did not know how to help athletes build relationships with each other and was overwhelmed by Mitchell's second assignment. After their last meeting, Coach War spent the day with his kids at the library. While they enjoyed story time with a magical princess named Julie, a middle-aged woman wearing a wig and a dress, he meandered through the self-help section. But after an hour of perusing books about relationships, Coach War was no better off.

The next day, he emailed the other coaches in his district, asking each what they did to build relationships in their programs. Only two coaches had responded. One response was from a well-known coach whom he respected because of the numerous district championship banners that hung in the rafters of their gym. His email was frank, saying that Coach War was wasting his time with "touchy-feely stuff," and his advice was to focus on being more consistent with his team's scheme.

The second email was more promising. It came from another coach who was about Coach War's age. "What we do in our program," Coach War read on his phone, "is host a team dinner on the Thursday before each game." Coach War shook his head. This was nothing new. *Doesn't everyone do a team dinner Thursday after practice?* He kept reading. "At dinner, we break our team up into groups of six to eight players. Sometimes it's by positions, sometimes it's by class, sometimes it's just random. Then, we give each table of players a question to discuss. Everyone must participate. Groups stick around after dinner until everyone has shared."

Coach War liked this idea. Eating has always been a natural time for humans to talk to each other. It reminded him of one of his favorite Warrington family traditions known as the "War Report." Each night at the dinner table, Laura would lead every member of the family as they shared what their day was like. Coach War always listened intently, like a four-star general receiving battle updates from his officers. He especially enjoyed hearing what his oldest daughter Maya was working on in school.

Mrs. Warrington would ask their toddler about her day, reading from the daily parent letter that was sent home from daycare. "Ella was happy," it might say with a smiley face circled. "Today she enjoyed…" and the day care would list various activities ranging from coloring to dress-up, with each one she participated in check-marked. She shared their infant son Max's day care note as well.

The nightly War Report was a fundamental part of Coach War's relationship with his own kids, and it helped him stay abreast with what was happening in their family. After all, Laura was the one mostly responsible for the emotional labor of the household. So, as Coach War read the email from his colleague, it made sense to him to try it with his football team. Setting his cell phone on the kitchen counter, he reached for a pen and scribbled "team dinner discussion" on a legal pad as one idea he was open to trying.

Chapter Thirteen

Relationships are a Team Effort

Coach War pushed open the heavy glass door, entering ChapaChino. The bottoms of his flip flops peeled off the floor with each step. He was in full summer mode, wearing navy-blue team shorts, a plain gray T-shirt, and his favorite "Titan Football" visor. He had a worn, black coaching bag slung over his left shoulder, swaying around his right hip as he walked to the booth in the back. Sitting down across from Mitchell, Coach War unzipped his bag to retrieve his yellow legal pad. Scribbled across the first page were several notes, with the most important concepts starred and circled.

"Well," Mitchell said, acknowledging Coach War's work, "I see you have done your homework." He was impressed with Coach War's due diligence and effort.

"This assignment was hard to do at first," Coach War began, "because I've never thought about it. I reached out to other coaches, did some research, and looked up some videos about how great companies build teams, and here is what I came up with." Coach War turned the legal pad so that it faced Mitchell, pointing to the bottom of the page. Written on the legal pad was a short list of three ideas that Coach War was willing to try with his team in the fall.

1. Circle Stretching – Create a "Titan Circle of Trust."
2. Dinner Discussions – Form groups and reflective questions to be discussed each week at Team Dinner.
3. Watch Monday Night Football together!

Mitchell looked over the list and smiled. He noticed how other ideas were scratched out and Coach War's notes filled the margins. Over the next hour, the two friends talked about the specifics of how to successfully embed each of these strategies next season. At the end of their time together, both were smiling. Coach War felt productive; Mitchell felt valued.

Chapter Fourteen

Pack Your Own Parachute

The next time Coach War met with Mitchell, it was after the 4th of July. Coach War's summer was quickly slipping away, each day falling like a grain of sand to the bottom of an hourglass. He had already begun preparing for the marathon of the upcoming season by working on several things that needed to be done before camp started next week. Coach War started his day prioritizing his to-do list by using psychologist Daniel Pink's "MIT" strategy. Looking at his lengthy list of annual responsibilities that he kept in a Google Drive folder, Coach War highlighted his "Most Important Task" for the day and knocked it out. The anxiety of the season was already starting to wear on him, and the stresses of leadership shackled his ankle like a ball and chain.

Mitchell observed a lack of mindfulness in Coach War this morning. Most of their meetings were comprised of easy conversation, but today Coach War was bouncing from topic to topic like a toddler experiencing their first sugar-high. Mitchell probed, but did not critique.

"So, Coach," Mitchell said between sips of his usual cappuccino, "when does your season start? It has to be coming up." His mind drifted back to his own coaching days. "I always thought the 4th of July signaled the end of my summer."

"Next week," Coach War said, nodding. His tone was flat and unenthusiastic.

"And are you ready?"

"I'm getting there. There's just so much to do," Coach War complained. "I've got paperwork for over ninety kids to track down and file, I need to nail down a photographer for picture day, and, if we want our gear to be in by the week of the first game, the team clothing order needs to be finalized and running by the end of the week." Coach War looked down, running his left hand through his hair. "And on top of all that, I'm worried about how I'm going to build relationships with all my players!"

Mitchell smiled and empathized with Coach War, remembering the preseason stress that came with the position of head football coach and the personal toll it took on the leader and his family.

"I love your prioritization strategy," Mitchell comforted. "Just keep going and remember… little by little, big things get done."

Coach War drew in a long breath, allowing himself to relax temporarily. He cleared his mind to be more present in their meeting. Mitchell noticed a teachable moment and asked Coach War a follow-up question.

"Do you know why you get paid to coach football?"

Coach War quickly considered Mitchell's question. "Because of all the extra time I spend at practice and on game day?"

"There's no doubt that coaching takes a ton of time, but you don't get paid for that. And the games are the fun part. Coach, you get paid for picture day."

Coach War did not understand; Mitchell elaborated.

"As a leader, it is your duty to be prepared… to take responsibility for things that have to get done. Coaches get paid for doing things that other people are unwilling to do."

Coach War had never thought about it that way before.

"You mean like organizing picture day?" Coach War questioned.

"Exactly!" Mitchell agreed. "Great example. No one *wants* to organize picture day, but it is part of your responsibilities. And, with every task you complete, you pack your own parachute." Mitchell paused to let this analogy sink in. "Think about paratroopers who jump out of an airplane into a combat zone."

Grainy black and white film from World War II archives flashed through Coach War's mind. He saw a heavy metal door being pulled open by an officer, exposing a gaping hole over thirty thousand feet of open atmosphere. The soldiers who had been sitting in the hull were ordered to rise and form a single-file line. Staring at his watch, the jumpmaster precisely timed each jump, and soldier after soldier made the plunge. Jumping was their job, not an option.

Mitchell continued.

"Each paratrooper carefully packs their own parachute *before* the mission. They meticulously check it as they pack and double-check it later to make sure everything is squared away. It's the dirty work that no one sees, and it has to be done *before* boarding the plane. The success of every mission hinges on each person's ability to pack their own parachute."

"Oh," Coach War said, grasping Mitchell's analogy, "so just like the paratroopers, I get paid to prepare."

"Correct! And one more thing, Coach. Take your time. Do not cut corners. Just like you wouldn't want to cut down trees with a dull axe, you wouldn't want to jump out of an airplane with an improperly packed parachute. Don't count on someone else to prepare *your* team. No one's going to pack your parachute for you."

As their last meeting for the summer ended, Coach War left ChapaChino more mindful about his coaching responsibilities. Mitchell's perspective reenergized him with a new purpose as he thought about his role as a leader. The bells on the entrance door jingled as Coach War pushed it open. He thought about his preseason to-do list. *The airplane is about to leave, and I've got more packing to do.*

Chapter Fifteen

"IT'S A GREAT DAY FOR FOOTBALL!"

Coach War was more excited than ever to start fall camp. His summer meetings with Mitchell had helped him sharpen his axe, and he was ready to hit the forest. Though the early August afternoon temperatures soared close to triple digits, Coach War threw on a light, short-sleeve "Titan Football" windbreaker to contrast his gray Nike shorts. His trademark black sunglasses rested on top of his head, giving him a fresh appearance. Coach War laced up his new, navy-blue Nike Free shoes and charged out of the field house as if his hair were on fire; his silver whistle swung rapidly from side to side around his neck as he sprinted toward the practice field. By the time he reached the corner of the end zone, sweat was pouring off his forehead. He felt invincible.

Most of the players were excited to be there too. Teammates wearing T-shirts and shorts gathered in small clumps around the goalpost. Some of the upperclassmen tossed a ball back and forth as they talked about their summers, cracking jokes. Incoming freshmen looked like fish out of water, standing off to the side, many of whom were apprehensive about playing high school football. Technically camp was optional, but everyone knew that if you wanted to play for the Titans, that camp was *practice* and it was *mandatory*. Legally, pads could not be worn until the next week, but Coach War's main concern wasn't player safety. He thought it was every athlete's job to prove their worth to the team. If that meant sacrificing their bodies for the greater good of the team, so be it.

Coach War lifted his silver whistle to his mouth, holding it in place with his teeth. He closed his eyes, imagining himself as the lumberjack ready to start a long day's work. He felt his chest rise as he drew in a deep breath. Coach War's shoulders tensed as he visualized the lumberjack lifting his heavy axe, ready to deliver a tree's first blow. Opening his eyes, he returned to the present. Air from his lungs pushed the small ball in the cavity of the metal whistle and a long, shrill sound pierced the atmosphere.

The players snapped to attention. They ran to their familiar stretching spots, falling into formation. Seniors were at the front of the platoon, while freshmen formed the caboose. Assistant coaches helped newcomers find a spot. Ten seniors claimed the front line, doing an about-face staring back at the younger "Boys of Fall." These ten would be the poster-boys for what a Titan football player was supposed to be. Coach War was pleased with his team's discipline on the first day of camp. In previous years, he would have used his stopwatch to time the team, charting their progress each day on a clipboard. But things were different this year. Two additional tugs on the whistle interrupted the traditional team stretch.

"Men," Coach War yelled, pacing the freshly cut grass in the middle of the formation, "this year we will shake things up from the way the way we've stretched before."

Assistant coaches looked at each other in wonder, unsure of what Coach was going to do.

"This year we will stretch in a giant circle between the hashes so you will be able to look your teammates in the eye. This will be our Titan Circle of Trust. Ready? Get to it." Coach War put his hands on his hips, watching as, line by line, players moved out of ranks and into a weird-looking formation that resembled a kidney bean.

"Holy crap, this is what you think a circle looks like?" Coach War razzed. "Someone go get Mr. Johnson to check our geometry!"

Some of the players laughed while the assistant coaches helped the guys even out their circle.

"From now on, this is where you will stretch," Coach War barked. "Remmy will lead you."

"Titan toe touches," Remmy announced. "Ready? Begin!"

"One, two, three, four, five, six, seven, eight, nine, ten!" they counted in unison. Two claps cued Remmy to transition to the next stretch.

Coach War stood in the center of the Titan Circle of Trust. He reached for the plastic page protector that was folded in his shorts, pressed against the small of his back. He slid the top paper out, then refolded the plastic sleeve and put it back in his shorts. Coach War stared at his roster, removing a pen that was clipped to the lanyard of his whistle. Another change this year was that Coach War would take attendance, a task he previously delegated to an assistant coach.

Mitchell's voice dashed through Coach War's mind as he clicked the pen and began to implement the first phase in The Process of the 'Ship. *Coach, relationships are essential. You cannot pursue victory with honor* until *you have captured the hearts of your athletes. And, if you don't purposefully work to build relationships with your athletes, the games are meaningless... even if you do win.*

The most basic element of any relationship begins with knowing someone's name. If Coach War *didn't* take attendance, how could he begin to get to know his athletes? There had to be at least ninety kids at Titans camp, over twenty of them freshmen. One by one, Coach War checked the names off his list. Each kid yelled "here!" after their name was called.

That wasn't so bad, Coach War reflected. *I can do that every day.*

As the team counted out the last stretch, Coach War blew his whistle, bringing the Titans together in a massive huddle. Remmy held his hand high in the center of the huddle to lead the traditional Titan breakdown.

"Titans on thr—"

Coach War interrupted the chant, pushing his way to the center of the circle of trust.

"From now on," he announced, "we will start each practice on my command." He pushed the inner circle back two steps to create more space. At the top of his lungs, he screamed with everything he had, "IT'S A GREAT DAY FOR FOOTBALL!"

The whistle blew long and hard. The Titan Circle of Trust erupted in cheers. Players sprinted to their individual position groups with purpose and energy, inspired to get the season rolling. Titan Football not only looked different, it *felt* different.

Chapter Sixteen

"TITAN WEATHER!"

Fall camp came and went, leading into official practice, then game week. While the defense had more installed than the offense, and executed more efficiently, that was to be expected. Overall, Coach War was pleased with his team's preseason progress. True to his word, every practice began with Coach War taking attendance and shouting, "IT'S A GREAT DAY FOR FOOTBALL!" amid the Titan Circle of Trust. Some days the sun beat down on the Boys of Fall mercilessly. On these days, Coach War invested more energy into managing his players' mindset and attitudes, since he could not control the weather. On Tuesday of game week, the toughest practice of the week, temperatures pushed the thermometer over one hundred degrees. Coach War stood looking directly into a westward wind that was pounding the boys like a furnace.

"What kind of weather is this!" he screamed.

"TITAN WEATHER!" the team yelled back.

Preparing in the heat added an element of toughness to Coach War's already grueling practice. After a long, physical practice, he knew that his boys were beat and that they would benefit from a boost of morale. The players formed a semi-circle around Coach War. While Coach War gave his practice notes to the team, his assistant coaches worked behind the kids' backs. Coach Roman unfolded two, twenty-by-twenty-foot blue rain tarps, staking them into the ground. Coach

Hogan unreeled a long hose from the water hydrant, stringing it out to the edge of the closest tarp. When they were done setting up, Coach Roman gave Coach War a big thumb's up.

"OK," Coach War said, looking down at his wristwatch. "You have ten minutes." He blew his whistle and pointed toward the tarps. Before the players could see what was happening, Coach Roman lifted the hose and covered its opening with his thumb. He pointed it toward the semi-circle and soaked as many kids as possible, laughing maniacally. A mass of players bull-rushed him, tackling him to the ground. They wrestled the hose away from him as more Titans formed a massive dog pile on the first blue tarp.

For the next few minutes, no one thought about football. The players ripped off their pads, stripping down to their girdles. One by one they sprinted ten yards before launching themselves onto the tarps, sliding at full speed on their backs and bellies. Coach War watched the chaos. He relished the linemen trying to one-up each other as they held a contest for who could slide the farthest. Their large, bare bellies glistened in the sun. Bursts of laughter erupted from the team as the two-hundred-plus-pound athletes slid wildly down the tarps, out of control. Coach War wasn't just building relationships anymore, he was capturing hearts.

Chapter Seventeen

"Titan Talk"

Thursday's practice was always "Play the Game Thursday" on the game field. Each week the Titan coaching staff created a mock game that included every situation their team could possibly face the next night. This was a vital part of preparing during game week, as it gave Coach War the ability for his players to mentally rehearse anything that could happen. Players looked forward to Thursday. The game plan was fully installed. Dress was light, just helmets and PE clothes, and practicing on the game field was special for the guys. Many of their dads had played for the Titans, and they grew up hearing stories about the Titan legacy.

"Don't take playing football for granted," they were told. "It's your responsibility to leave the program in a better place than when you got there." After all, you never know what play will be your last.

In the final moments of the mock game, a whistle blew from behind the kicker as a ball was placed on a tee at the forty-yard line. Standing ten yards away, the Titan hands team was eagerly waiting to do its job by successfully recovering the onside kick from Coach Roman; they did. The offense jogged onto the field.

"Time for the greatest play in football," Coach War preached in the huddle. "Just hold onto the ball."

The snap count echoed throughout the empty stadium as the offense prepared for one more play on the line of scrimmage.

"Ready. Set. Hit!"

The center snapped the ball to the signal caller, who dropped back three steps. Two split backs squeezed in close, providing extra protection, just in case.

"Ah," Coach War said casually to Coach Roman as his quarterback took a knee, "is there anything in the world more beautiful than the victory formation?"

He blew the game's final whistle. Players cheered, slapping each other on the butts and backs as if they had just won an actual game. The offense jogged to the sideline, joining their teammates in the single-file line on the Titans' side of the fifty-yard line for the traditional postgame handshake. Everything was rehearsed.

After high-fiving imaginary opponents, the players met Coach War at the twenty-five yard line, forming the Titan Circle of Trust around him. Each Titan took a knee, keeping their lids on, waiting to be briefed on the game day schedule. When the last Titan joined the circle, Coach War pulled his small notebook out of the back of his pants and addressed his team.

"Tomorrow, you need to be at the high school by five p.m. You need to be dressed and ready to go by five thirty. Skill guys will be on the field at 5:35 and linemen will come out at 5:50. Kickoff is at seven. Any questions?"

Some players started to unbuckle their chinstraps, ready to lift the helmets off their heads. Coach War paused, shooting his restless players the teacher's look; all movement ceased.

"Team dinner will be in the high school cafeteria tonight. This week, the seniors' parents are feeding you. Make sure that you say thank you as you go through the line. Seniors, you will eat first." Coach War glanced at his notes in the spiral notebook. He needed to tell his team about the new team dinner discussion but could not decide on how to do it. In the end, he opted to speak from the heart.

"Some of you have noticed some changes we've made at practice." The seniors nodded toward the juniors. "Well, we're making some changes with the team dinner also. When you go through the food line, you will pick a table to sit at. The first person can pick any table. The next person has to pick a new table. And so it will go until every table has one person sitting at it. The next person in line can then sit at any table, and the process will continue until everyone is seated."

The players grumbled. They had always been able to eat with their buddies.

"Also," Coach War instructed, "while you eat, you will have a discussion question to talk about with your teammates. The questions will vary from week to week. I call this 'Titan Talk.' Everyone will participate. When someone in your group shares, you need to look them in the eye and listen, I mean *really listen* to what they are saying. This isn't think-pair-share bullshit in Mrs. Riley's Biology class. Got it?"

The upperclassmen laughed.

"Got it?" Coach War reiterated, this time with more urgency in his tone.

"Yes, sir!" the team responded in unison.

"Good. Your first Titan Talk discussion question is… what do you like most about playing football?" Coach War knew he was starting small, but at least he was trying. "Gentlemen," he said in closing, "see you in the cafeteria."

Chapter Eighteen

Laugh, Don't Like

At first, Titan Talk was a bust. Awkwardness engulfed the cafeteria as the players moved through the food line. Seeing his team struggling with the new activity, Coach War jumped in. His booming voice filled the room, commanding his team's attention.

"Gentlemen," he bellowed. "Many of you don't know how to begin, so I will go first. What I like most about football is game day. There is *no* day like game day! I love seeing the hallway filled with blue jerseys on Fridays in the fall. I love our school pep rallies where the pep band gets everyone hyped by playing songs like "All I Do Is Win" by DJ Khaled. And most of all, I love leading the charge onto the field under the Friday night lights. That's a rush you can't get anywhere else." Coach War looked around the room, making eye contact with his players as he moved from table to table. "Now, I expect you to look at the teammates who are sitting at your table and share your favorite part of playing football too. The oldest person at your table will go first."

The quiet room slowly grew louder as more and more Titans shared. Seeing Coach War open up made it easier for the players to offer their perspectives. Coach War paced from table to table, observing the scene, making mental notes for how it could be better. He was pleased to see upper and lower classmen sitting together, each contributing to the group conversation. Coach War listened in to what his athletes liked most about the greatest sport in the world.

"Football allows me to hit someone else… legally," one player mentioned.

"I feel powerful when the ball is in my hand… it's like I'm invincible," another player sitting at another table shared. Coach War heard a freshman speak next.

"I was really nervous about starting high school, but once football started, I made some new friends, and that helped me on the first day of school."

Coach War was pleased with the first installment of Titan Talk. The parents were pleased as well. Nearly every senior parent who was there to serve team dinner complimented Coach War on this change, saying that they wished he would have done this when their son was a freshman.

Again, Mitchell's words turned in his mind. *Little by little, big things get done.*

* * *

The Titans played well in their season opener the following night. The locker room erupted as the team celebrated a lopsided home win. "Get Low" by Lil Jon blared amid a circle of players, who took turns in the center for a brief solo dance. When the chorus hit, they all threw their hands in the air and screamed.

"From the windooowww… to the wall!"

Coach War tried to remain incognito, discretely keeping his head down as he passed his players on his way to the coaches' office. But he was discovered and sucked into the high energy chaos. As Dabo Swinney believes, when you win, you dance. Coach War did his best sprinkler, then progressed to the lawn mower, before finishing with a sloppy version of the Macarena.

Coach Hogan turned to Coach Roman just outside of the coaches' office and asked, "Is Coach *dancing* or having a seizure?"

The players loved Coach War's moves. The athletes cheered a loud abrupt "Hey!" to the fast-paced song as he did his best to keep up with the beat. The Titans were enjoying the moment together. Coach Roman could see that Coach War was stuck, so he tossed an imaginary fishing line toward the circle. Coach War took the bait. He stuck his index finger in the corner of his mouth before flopping like a fish out of the circle. Coach Roman reeled him in.

In the coaches' office, Coach War's heart was content. He slumped in his usual spot on the couch, letting his body relax and his mind process what had happened. Loud screams and music thumped against the heavy steel door. Coach War began the usual postgame routine, which was always the same, win or lose. Tonight, however, winning felt different. It felt *meaningful.*

Coach War unlocked his phone screen, clicking on the blue bird pinned to the bottom of his iPhone. He wanted to tweet out the final score on the Titan Football Twitter account while his laptop uploaded the night's game film. Before he could click on the pen and paper icon to start a tweet, his timeline showed its most recent post, written by one of his players. He read it silently to himself.

"Ding ding ding! We loud AF tonight!" the athlete scribed, a reference to the Titans' tradition of ringing the victory bell after each win.

Right on, Coach War thought. *Winning should be fun. My team is finally buying in.*

He smiled, liking the post before retweeting it, and forwarding it on for fans of the program to revel in. When the game film was ready, he uploaded it to the team's online Hudl library. He thanked his assistants for a great night, then sent them home. After a few minutes the file had completely downloaded. Coach War reached for his legal pad and a pen and settled into the coaches' office couch to watch the eye in the sky, which never lies, ready to take notes for Monday's team meeting in Coach Hogan's room.

Late in the first half of the film, a knock on the door interrupted Coach War's concentration.

"Come in, it's open," he yelled through the door, unsure of who was knocking or how late it really was. Mr. Allen twisted the door handle and stepped inside office. He closed the door behind him.

"Coach," Mr. Allen began, "good win tonight."

"Thanks," Coach War responded. "Our kids played hard."

"I agree. The team looks much improved." Mr. Allen paused before explaining the reason for his visit. "Coach, we need to talk about a tweet you sent out from the program's account."

Coach War looked up from his computer screen; he was confused. "What's wrong with posting the score of the game?"

"Nothing," Mr. Allen replied. "In fact, I like how you engage Titan fans by posting final scores. The issue I have is with a post from a player that you retweeted."

"Oh," Coach War groaned, remembering his timeline. "What's wrong with it?"

"For starters, it contains some offensive language. You can use Urban Dictionary to get the specifics, but your tweet has received some negative attention. Now, I'm not going to tell you that you *can't* use social media, but you need to understand what you post and that it can get you fired."

Mr. Allen looked Coach War directly in the eyes and lowered his voice. "I need you to delete your post. Pronto."

Coach War complied. He withdrew his iPhone from the pocket of his khaki shorts and deleted the player's post from the Titan Football account's timeline.

"Thank you," Mr. Allen said, stepping back. "I'll let you get some work done. I suggest you talk to your team about how to use social media *appropriately* in the future."

Coach War nodded.

"And, in the future, Coach, when you see a post that uses that kind of language, my advice would be to laugh, but don't like it or forward it on."

Mr. Allen closed the steel door to the coaches' office behind him, leaving Coach War to watch film in solitude.

Chapter Nineteen

Monday Night Football

Aside from game day, Coach War's favorite day of the week was Monday thanks to Monday Night Football. When he was a young boy, his father used the weekly telecast to instill a love for the game while bonding with his son. A small, boxy television occupied the living room corner of his childhood home. Reception was limited. Vinny Warrington was the remote control. Mr. Warrington would nudge him in the ribs when it was time to turn the channel or adjust the volume. Vinny would get up, walk over to the set, and turn the two simple dials that loudly clicked into place. Bunny ears caked in tin foil extended toward the ceiling and needed constant readjusting; Vinny did that too. The Warringtons' TV only received three basic channels—ABC, NBC, and CBS—and Mr. Warrington would not tolerate anything other than the news.

"Damn it," he would complain to his wife, "I don't go to work every day so our kids can be entertained by Captain Kangaroo! If they are going to watch something, it's going to be educational. They've got to know what's going on in the world!" Mr. Warrington still lived in fear of political tension as the Iron Curtain slowly descended and the Cold War drew to a close.

Monday nights, however, were the exception. Mr. Warrington *loved* football, especially when the Packers were on. He was a blue-collar worker from the steel belt, like his father, who identified with the blue-collar team. While other NFL teams were from major US cities and had multi-million-dollar stadiums, Mr. Warrington appreciated the small town of Green Bay, Wisconsin, whose livelihood depended on the meat packing industry. Mr. Warrington was smitten by Vince Lombardi's no-nonsense, tough love, West Point discipline and drill sergeant leadership style. He was a boy when the Packers won Super Bowl I and Super Bowl II, and Vince Lombardi's legacy was untouchable. In the Warrington house at least, Lombardi's name was next to God's and *not* to be taken in vain.

Vinny's parents were just out of high school when they got married, and within the first three months of their life together Mrs. Warrington became pregnant. They talked endlessly about names for Baby Warrington, but two names stood above the rest. If the baby was a boy, he would be named Vincent, in honor of Mr. Warrington's favorite coach. On the other hand, if the baby was a girl, she would be named Starr, in honor of Bart Starr, the Packers legendary quarterback. In the end, Baby Warrington was a boy and, as promised, was named Vincent; Vinny for short.

Monday Night Football kicked off each week after eight p.m. central time, well past little Vinny's bedtime. Tip-toeing down the hall of their modest three-bedroom split-level, his dad would gently wake his young son, who would spring to life and run to the living room. Vinny would grab a pillow off the couch, then plop down as close to the TV as his dad would allow. He would watch the game each week sprawled out on the carpet in his He-Man pajamas.

Week after week, Vinny soaked it all in, listening to Howard Cosell on the call as he learned the game. His dad would relax on the family's couch, doing his best to quench his son's thirst for the "X's" and "O's." The Warringtons' refrigerator was always stocked with Pabst Blue Ribbon. Throughout the game during commercial breaks, Mr. Warrington would hold his empty can high, giving it a shake, letting the drink's last sips slosh back and forth against its aluminum wall. Vinny would spring into action, running to the kitchen to bring the next round. He always challenged himself to be back in his place on the carpet before that commercial was over.

This weekly ritual was a good deal for each of them. Vinny got to stay up late, while his dad had a personal servant for the evening; they both enjoyed the football. Of course, Vinny's mom discouraged this tradition, worrying that he would be too tired for school the next day. But Monday nights actually energized him. On Tuesdays at recess, Vinny would imitate his gridiron heroes in a pick-up game of Smear in the Clear, running back and forth as the other boys tried to tackle him. Mr. Warrington passed a few years back, broken from a long life of manual labor, but the Monday night memories Vinny and his dad shared lived on. Coach War hoped to share this tradition with his own son.

In high school athletics, Monday night means JV football. The dismissal bell echoed down the high school hallway at three p.m. sharp. A mass of bodies flooded the arteries of the school, darting around before spilling into the student parking lot. Some kids waited for the bus, sitting on small garden benches, while those old enough to drive and fortunate enough to have a car clogged the lot's main entrance. Music blared, horns honked, and kids yelled out of one car window into another. Part of the student body remained in school, however, making their way to the various club organizations they belonged to.

The JV players reported to the Titan locker room immediately after the bell. They found their jersey number in a giant stack of jerseys and grabbed an appropriately sized pair of pants off the equipment room counter. Players sat at their lockers, transferring their insert pads into their game pants before dressing for the game. The JV coaches prowled throughout the locker room, making themselves available to tape ankles and go over any part of the game plan the sophomores might have a question about.

The varsity football players, on the other hand, met in Coach Hogan's Social Studies classroom for film study. Coach Hogan's room was close to the field house, and the players reveled in the chance that they might see a volleyball girl outside the gym. The boys lingered, just for a moment, hoping to catch a glimpse of one of the girls in the tight black spandex shorts that were part of the volleyball uniform. The tape rolled at 3:15 sharp. Anyone who did not make the 3:15 start time would be locked out of the room, forced to wait in the locker room for the team to finish. These kids would have to face the wrath of Coach War, and no girl was hot enough to risk that.

Coach Hogan's room was dark. The projector hummed, powering the only visible light, which partly illuminated thirty desks organized into five rows of six. The Hudl playlist was cued up on the white board, ready to roll when the kids walked in. Coach Hogan ran Hudl from behind his desktop computer, while Coach War addressed the team with his thoughts from the game and notes accompanying the cut-up video clips. Standing like a statue, Coach War submerged himself into the darkness of the back of the room, ready to present from behind the last row of student desks. He stared at his watch until it flashed 3:14:50, and then the countdown began.

"Ten, nine, eight, seven, six, five, four..." he would say before holding up three fingers on his hand like a cameraman facilitating a live TV show. The players would continue counting.

"Three, two, one!" they would crescendo.

"The eye in the sky doesn't lie," he would say, before yelling. "Now let's get better!" This was Coach Hogan's cue to start the first clip.

The Hudl playlist was a compilation of plays from the previous Friday night. Over the weekend, Titan coaches were expected to insert their comments directly onto Hudl, starring the plays they would like to show their position groups. Playlists included positive plays as well as things the team needed to improve; there were always more positive comments after a win. Coach War's eyes had the focus of his laser pointer; he watched the film like a hawk. Coach Hogan would rewind plays over and over, or put them in slow motion, as Coach War demanded. He wanted to make sure his players got the point.

After all the comments had been doled out, Coach War would give a scouting report for the Titans' upcoming game, showing a few cut-ups of the opponent's offensive and defensive tendencies. Film study was long, usually at least an hour, and players were expected to keep their focus. Any player who was off-task, or worse, caught sleeping, was banished to the locker room. Once the film session was over, varsity athletes were released to the weight room for a short lift and their only early night home that week.

Coach Roman would appear to personally escort the players to the weight room. In addition to his responsibilities as an assistant coach, Coach Roman was the Titans' strength and conditioning coordinator. Anything that had to do with the weight room, no matter what sport was in season, was in Coach Roman's jurisdiction.

"This is my territory, son," Coach Roman would say about the large strength and conditioning complex attached to the field house. "I've pissed in all four corners."

"Just hold on a sec," Coach War said, holding up his right hand like a crossing guard stopping oncoming traffic. "Tonight, the JV has their first game… they're home. Make sure you get down to the field and support them. Also, starting tonight, every Monday I will be hosting a Monday night meeting." Coach War paused while his players groaned. "It's not that kind of meeting," he clarified. "The Jets play the Dolphins on Monday Night Football. I will buy pizza and Gatorade for anyone who wants to come over and watch it with my family."

The players looked around the room at each other sheepishly.

"There's no catch," Coach War continued. "Just come over and watch football and have a good time." Coach War stepped back as the players huddled around Coach Roman.

"Titans on three," yelled Remmy. "One, two, three…"

"TITANS!" the team barked, then departed for the weight room.

Chapter Twenty

"Titan Night Football"

Six players accepted Coach War's Monday Night Football invitation. He was hoping for more, but six was a start. Tuesday morning Coach War found himself scouting the Titans' next opponent on his iPad as he waited for Mitchell. Ironically, Mitchell had been standing in the doorway for a good two minutes as Coach War stared at the small screen. Mitchell's rapping on the coaches' office steel door made Coach War jump, snapping him out of his zombie-like trance.

"Oh good, you're alive," Mitchell teased, sitting down on the couch in his usual spot.

"Sorry, how long have you been standing there?" Coach War rubbed his eyes.

"Not a terrible amount of time, but long enough for my knees to begin to swell." Mitchell tugged at each of his knees, first the right, then the left, lifting them off the ground.

"So," he grunted, "how is the season going?"

"Well," Coach War retorted cheerfully, "we are off to a great start, 1-0."

"I see. And the relationship-building? The hmmm… Process of the 'Ship?" Mitchell twirled his hand in the air as he recalled the first phase in his winning formula.

"Actually, great! It's easier than I thought it would be. Making minor changes to the things we already do is beginning to pay dividends."

Over the course of the next hour, the two friends talked about practice, Coach War's team, and Monday Night Football, brainstorming ways that would help Coach War improve relationships and lead with a sharper axe.

The second week of Monday Night Football featured the Broncos at the Raiders, a classic AFL rivalry. Eight Titans accepted Coach War's open invitation for pizza and football… the original six members plus two newcomers. The game played on the fifty-inch flatscreen that was mounted above the fireplace as the Warrington kids ran wildly around the house. The high school students lifted the little ones onto their shoulders, flying them around the living room like airplanes. At the end of the first quarter, Laura rounded them up to take them to bed. Even the high school kids complained.

"Ah, but Mrs. Warrington," Remmy begged, "just a *little* longer?"

"Sorry—it's a school night. I guess I'm the fun-hater. You'll have to wait until next week." And that was the end of that. Coach War had gotten used to getting the *second* to last word a long time ago. He chuckled at the look on Remmy's face when she whisked all three kids down the hall, as only a mom could do, and put them to bed for the evening.

By the third week, Monday Night Football had become a huge success. The players even started calling it "Titan Night Football." They held a weekly contest for the game's biggest hit, something they called "The Hit of the Week." Every Titan could claim one hit throughout the game, and *only* if they saw it first. At the end of the night, the group would vote on whose hit was the most explosive. The winner earned preferential seating on the leather sectional for next week's game. Winning "The Hit of the Week" contest became competitive. Players who won would show up the next week and treat the reclining leather seat like a throne. One of the juniors even made a paper-mache crown in art class to be given as a traveling trophy from week to week.

The guys would talk about Titan Night Football at school on Tuesdays, and the number of attendees grew throughout the season. By the fourth week, the Warringtons' living room was standing room only. JV players would come over after their game and watch the second half. The Titans created a fantasy football league so they could further challenge each other. Winning the fantasy league came with the prize of having the other members serve the winner for a week at lunch. Conversely, the person who came in last would have to stand up in front of the school and sing "Barbie Girl" in the commons. Coach War laughed as he wrote out the agreed-upon terms on a piece of paper from his legal pad. After every member of Titan Night Football had signed the document, Coach War taped it next to the TV on the living room wall.

"Really?" Laura contested.

"Really. C'mon, the guys love it. Just for the season," Coach War promised.

Laura relented. It was now officially a living, breathing, iron-clad, legally-binding document. No exceptions. Whenever Coach War looked at the paper hanging on his living room wall, he wished it was Monday. His players' excitement for Monday Night Football took him back to when he was a kid with his father. Now, as an adult, Coach War couldn't wait for Titan Night Football.

Chapter Twenty-One

Rivalry Game

After starting the season 4-0, it was Lone Tree week. Lone Tree was a football powerhouse thirty minutes down Titan Drive. They were the Titans' primary rival, but it was a one-sided affair. Lone Tree had hoisted thirteen state championship banners in school history, five of which had come during Coach Warrington's time with the Titans. Hell, the Titans didn't have thirteen *district* championships and had never even *played* for a state title. Still, Coach War was confident heading into the matchup.

On game day, the school burst with Titan Pride all day. At the morning pep rally, the band put everyone on their feet by playing "Crazy Train," followed by the school song. Mr. Allen facilitated the event, and Coach War was the main speaker. While the players loved the pep rallies, the coaches found them distracting, draining valuable energy.

When the team finally loaded the bus at four p.m. to drive to Lone Tree, Coach War was exhausted. He was the last one to board, taking attendance on the stoop of the bus stairs. He confirmed that everyone was indeed on the bus, then used the metal railing to climb the stairs, plopping down on the first green, canvas covered seat he saw. The team was silent as the bus pulled around the flagpole, rolling south on Titan Drive toward Lone Tree. Coach War glanced back, looking down the aisle as the bus reached its top highway speed. Bright-blue headphones bridged many of his players' ears as they stared forward in silence. *Man, Dr. Dre is killing it with his Beats,* he thought, wanting to take a power nap. Instead, Coach War pulled out his laminated call sheet and made the final adjustments, writing notes in the margin with a Sharpie.

It was a perfect night for football. Hamburgers and hot dogs sizzling on a large grill by the concession stand filled the darkening evening air with a smoky haze; tailgating smells wafted through the grandstand. The game proved to be as good as the atmosphere. At halftime, it was tied at fourteen. The Titans crammed into the girls' locker room, which was also used as the visitors' locker room at Lone Tree High. The clacking sound of their cleats scraping the concrete floor popped off the bare brick walls. One by one they sat on a long, narrow wooden bench, taking swigs out of the team water bottles. Steam hovered over the players' heads, fogging up the locker room mirrors. Coach War conferred with his assistant coaches before addressing his team. The players leaned in to hear his words.

"OK, men. Pretty good half out there. This is right where we want to be. We're moving the ball and playing mistake free. We need to keep that up in the second half. Trust that good things will continue to happen." Coach War stepped aside, allowing the offensive and defensive coordinators to address the team and make the agreed upon adjustments that would help the Titans prevail. When they had finished, Coach War resumed. "We get the ball to start the second half. Now's our opportunity! Take control of this game, and make them suck the hind tit! Let's go!"

Players hooped and hollered as they charged out of the locker room, jogging onto a white rock trail that wound around the back of the school, leading to the game field. The players were motivated, but their self-control had yet to be tested. Coach War mulled the situation over with Coach Roman as the players stretched on the sideline in preparation for the second half.

"Wow," Coach Roman said, "they are hype!"

Coach War narrowed his eyes.

"Too hype. I don't know if we're strong enough mentally to handle the pressure of this game."

Coach Roman agreed.

"Lone Tree will come out swinging in the second half. I just hope our kids will respond."

Coach War's fears were confirmed when the Titans fumbled the second half kickoff, giving Lone Tree a short field, which led to a touchdown. Fielding the next kickoff, the Titan offense was unable to move the ball, going three and out. With their back against the wall, the punter's heels were barely ahead of the goal line. A beautiful punt out-kicked the coverage, spiraling past midfield. Lone Tree's returner tracked the ball that soared beyond the lights, cupped it as it landed, then turned on the gas, hitting full stride as he weaved his way through traffic all the way to the end zone. In what seemed like a blink of an eye, Lone Tree's momentum had propelled them to a commanding 28-14 lead. The Titans never recovered, trailing 42-14 late in the fourth quarter.

Coach War prowled the sideline like a caged tiger. He directed his frustration at the side judge. "That's a block in the back," he pleaded to deaf ears as Lone Tree again marched down field. "There's a hold!" he exclaimed on the next play, directly at the official. "C'mon! You can't let them get away with that!" Coach War's reptilian brain reached the point where he was no longer coaching his team. He was only interested in the closest referee, hoping he would pity the Titans and throw his team a bone.

When the Titans drew a penalty, jumping off-sides, Coach War hung his head. The situation escalated. The head official picked up the ball, moving the line of scrimmage closer to the Lone Tree end zone. The head official marked off *six* yards instead of the five by rule. The head official made eye contact with Coach War, then winked.

Coach War stalked the side judge, chirping in his ear.

"What! Did you really just penalize us *six* yards!"

"Coach, I didn't touch the ball," the side judge responded with his whistle clenched between his teeth, his eyes forward, fixed on the line of scrimmage.

"That's fucking bullshit! Who's paying you?" Coach War demanded. "Are you a Lone Tree grad or just a local homer?" He turned his head away briefly, letting a stream of spit land on the ground. Coach War was unable to focus on the next play. "Holy shit that's a terrible call!"

The official looked at Coach War, unable to ignore his behavior anymore. Running onto the field from the sideline, the side judge jerked a mustard-yellow flag out from under his belt, hurling it back at Coach War. He ducked, avoiding the flag that was on a collision course for the side of his face. The side judge met the white hat at midfield, whispering in his ear. Dropping his flag to the turf, the head referee held his arms straight out, parallel to the ground, palms facing down.

"Unsportsmanlike conduct, Titans," he spoke into the stadium mic. "Fifteen-yard penalty. Automatic first down." The official dropped his left arm, making a tomahawk-like chop forward with his right. He signaled to the sideline for the chain crew to move the sticks.

Coach War threw his headset, running onto the field to protest the call. The Lone Tree pep band seized the opportunity to play Justin Timberlake's hit song "Can't Stop the Feeling!" Coach Roman chased after Coach War, catching up to him and locking his arms around his waist in a tight bear hug. Coach Roman lifted Coach War off the ground, carrying him to the opposite end of the Titans' sideline, where he spent the final minutes of the game standing in solitude, furiously chomping his gum. Lone Tree scored one more time, jamming the final dagger in the Titans' heart, as they cruised to another lop-sided victory over the Titans, 49-14.

Chapter Twenty-Two

Be Defendable

You could hear a pin drop in the Titans' locker room when the team returned to their school. The players moved like zombies, unpacking their travel bags at the foot of their lockers. They threw their dirty game jerseys and pants in a pile before leaving for the weekend. Coach War isolated himself in the coaches' office, alone with his thoughts, waiting for everyone to go home. He traded out his navy-blue "Titans Football" polo and khakis for a hoodie and sweatpants. He was unlacing his tennis shoes when there was a knock at the door. Coach War sat still, hiding like a possum playing dead. Another knock pounded at the steel, this time louder and more intense. Again, Coach War did not move.

Keys jingled from the other side of the locked door. A brief scratching noise drew Coach War's intense stare. He saw the button on the door handle pop out of its locked position before the door swung open, and Mr. Allen stepped in. Coach War dropped his eyes and head. He had been dreading this moment, but knew it was inevitable.

"Tough game tonight, Coach." Mr. Allen eased into the couch, crossing his legs. It was eerie how much he resembled Mitchell.

No shit, Coach War thought, wishing Mr. Allen would just hand down his punishment already.

"Well, I'm sure you know why I'm here, and you're probably not in a very good mood, so I'll just give it to you straight." Mr. Allen uncrossed his legs, moving to the edge of the couch. Staring into Coach War's eyes, he continued. "Coach, based on your sideline behavior tonight, the school administration has decided to suspend you for the next game."

"What!" Coach War screamed, rising out of his chair. "That's bullshhhhhh…"

Coach War noticed Mr. Allen raise an eyebrow, so he stopped himself from swearing, but he was livid.

"That's not fair! Next week is homecoming!" Coach War hurled his left Nike Free against the steel door of the coaches' office.

"The timing of this incident makes this harder," Mr. Allen agreed, "but there's no excuse for your behavior tonight. The officiating crew was ready to throw you out of the game. I had to talk them out of it. If they had thrown you out, you'd be suspended next week anyway. *Plus*, you would have to pay for the sportsmanship class that must be completed before you could coach again, *and* there would be a written reprimand in your coaching file. This suspension is the best option for all parties involved."

Coach War sat down on the couch next to Mr. Allen. He knew he was right. They sat for a long moment in silence together. Mr. Allen waited for Coach War's anger to dissipate.

"Look, Coach, accept the consequences for your behavior. Own it. Serve your suspension, and we'll move on together."

Coach War was disappointed, but he agreed to serve his suspension. Mr. Allen got up and opened the coaches' office door. The door swung inward, and Mr. Allen took two steps in the doorway before spinning back around to face Coach War.

"I've always defended you," he said in a somber voice, "because you've always been defendable, until tonight. We can get past this, but from now on, you have to be defendable again. Understand?"

Coach War nodded. Mr. Allen stepped into the Titans' locker room, gently closing the door behind him. Coach War rubbed his face with both of his palms, thinking in the stillness. *Suspended. I can't believe it. I've never been suspended.*

Chapter Twenty-Three

"Firetruck"

School spirit soars during homecoming week. Students and staff participate in themed dress-up days, attend daily pep rallies, and compete in class games, which the seniors *always* win. Students look forward to the annual activities put on by the student council throughout the week. The Powder Puff football game is on Monday. Girls form flag-football teams and ask Titan football players to coach them up. On Tuesday night, boys don headbands and black spandex to play in Volleyboy, an intramural volleyball tournament. Thursday brings the school and community together for a pep rally and bonfire, and homecoming culminates on Friday. Friday morning, the king and queen are announced during an all-school assembly, immediately followed by the town's parade. The Titan band marches amid floats from student clubs and organizations. People line both sides of Titan Drive, and children rush to recover any candy that is thrown in their direction. The parade concludes at the Titan Tailgate back in the high school parking lot. Students play bean bags and toss footballs, enjoying music and free food before kickoff. The homecoming dance after the game completes the week.

* * *

Mitchell was at school first thing Monday morning. It was Hawaiian Day for the Titans. Coach War taught in flip flops, board shorts, and a floral pattern polo, hiding behind dark aviator sunglasses. By now, word about his suspension was going around town and school. Mitchell was early for their weekly meeting, and it surprised Coach War to see him sitting on the couch in the coaches' office before the bell rang. Coach War removed his aviators, folding each of the ear holders, clipping the glasses to his shirt.

"So, Coach, how've you been?"

Coach War wondered how to answer that, unsure if Mitchell knew about what happened at Lone Tree; he hesitated.

"Not well," he responded.

"Not well because of the result of last week's game, or not well because of your suspension?" Mitchell was blunt, but genuinely curious, recognizing another teachable moment.

"Both, I guess," Coach War acknowledged. "So you know about what happened?"

"Yes, that's why I'm here today and not tomorrow," Mitchell confirmed. "Mr. Allen and I talked over the weekend."

Coach War paused, narrowing his eyes as he looked at Mitchell.

"Well don't you think a suspension is a *little* harsh? After all," Coach War justified, "I wasn't even kicked out of the game."

"No, but you could've been." Mitchell eased back into the couch. "I can see it from both perspectives, but I think a suspension is fair."

"What? Fair! The officials penalized us *six* yards on an offsides call. Don't you think I have the right to be angry?"

"Angry? Sure," Mitchell reasoned, his voice wavering. "But when your emotion goes high, your intelligence goes low."

"What would *you* have done?" Coach War asked, his tone short and to the point.

"Not much," Mitchell said.

"So I'm not supposed to fight for my team… just let it happen?"

"That's right. You're *not* supposed to fight for your team. You're supposed to *model* for your team." Mitchell waited, allowing Coach War to process this idea. "It's simple," he continued. "Your behavior was below the line. Your emotions were high, and your reaction was your default response. You allowed your frustration to get the best of you. Are you familiar with E + R = O?"

Coach War nodded. "Event, plus reaction, equals outcome. We use that a lot with our players. It helps our kids focus on the things they can control."

"Good," Mitchell praised. "It's important for teenagers to know that formula. However, it's even more important for people in leadership positions. Leaders must make a conscious choice to respond *above* the line, all the time. You cannot resort to your default behavior, even if it's justifiable. When adversity hits, leaders have to be willing to take the high road, especially when it's not easy or when you don't want to."

"So *that's* why I am suspended," Coach War concluded.

"You modeled to your team that it's OK to complain and blame the refs, and you did it with highly offensive language." Coach War hung his head, ashamed of how his emotions had been out of control. "All you can do is learn from this suspension and not repeat this behavior. And, Coach," Mitchell mused, standing up to leave the coaches' office as their session came to a close, "the only word *I know* that starts in 'f' and ends in 'u-c-k' is firetruck."

Chapter Twenty-Four

No Excuses

Each year Coach War looked forward to homecoming. This year, however, he found it hard to have school spirit or joke around with the students. He felt better after talking with Mitchell, but it was still hard to accept the fact that he would not be on the sideline Friday night. *Fake it until you feel it*, he told himself, trying to remain strong on his way to film study in Coach Hogan's room. This was the first time he had to face his team since Friday night.

"Fellas," he began, looking around the room, "it's homecoming week. Enjoy it, but remember… you have more to lose than the average student. Don't do anything that will jeopardize our mission on Friday night. That means *no Volleyboy!*"

Groans filled the classroom, but Coach War was emphatic.

"Remember, homecoming is all about a football game, and it's meaningless without a 'W.' Secondly, I want to start this week's preparation by apologizing for my behavior on Friday night. I let my emotions get the best of me. I should have never yelled at the officials like that. I'm sorry."

The players turned to each other grumbling.

"But, Coach," Remmy interjected, "you were right, it *was* BS! How's it OK that they can just mark off six yards? They can't do that to us!"

All of the others agreed with Remmy.

"Guys," Coach War assured, quieting his team, "I appreciate your support, but I was wrong. My emotion was too high." He pointed toward the ceiling with his right hand. "As a result, my intelligence was too low." Coach War dropped his hand, pointing toward the floor. "It's never OK to berate an official. I embarrassed myself and all of you. I'm man enough to admit when I'm wrong. Again, I'm sorry. It won't happen again. But there's still one thing I need to tell you."

More grumbling came from the players, unsure of what Coach War would say next.

"I've been suspended for this week's homecoming game. Coach Roman will—"

Again, Remmy spoke up.

"They can't do that! That's a bunch of horseshit! We'll go see Mr. Allen right now!"

The room erupted. Players rose out of their desks, making their way toward the door. Coach War was motionless, staring at his players.

"You will not… none of that," he spoke, quieting the small uprising. "I've agreed to the suspension. I want you to see that when you do something wrong, you need to take responsibility for it. I don't want you to make excuses, so I'm not making any for myself."

"So you won't be around at all this week?" Remmy asked.

"I will be with you at practice. We will prepare as normal for homecoming. Coach Roman will be the head coach on Friday night. He will make all decisions. I can't be on the sideline during the game, but I can be in the locker room before the game and at half. I will watch the game from the press box and rejoin you in the locker room for the postgame homecoming win celebration."

"Oh yeah," Remmy interrupted. "You can count on that!"

Clapping, hooting, and hollering filled Coach Hogan's classroom. Coach War smiled. He thought he had captured the hearts of his athletes, but now he knew it. He had taken the time necessary to win the locker room, and his players had his back. That's all he needed.

"All right then," Coach War said, smiling as he turned on the projector. "Let's get to work."

Chapter Twenty-Five

The Second Phase: Leadership

The Titans won a close homecoming game on a last second field goal as time expired. "Another One Bites the Dust," by Queen, blared as the players danced in the locker room. Coach War stormed in, slamming the heavy steel door of the coaches' office. One player immediately unplugged the stereo, and everyone stopped what they were doing. The room fell silent. Coach War took his time walking to the center of the locker room, his sneakers squeaking against the concrete floor with every step. When he reached the center, he hesitated, casting his steely gaze around the room. You could have heard a pin drop.

"I'm back!" he yelled, raising his hands toward the ceiling.

The room erupted. The Titans had never seen their coach smile so big. The stereo was plugged back into the wall, and loud thumping music resumed. The players jumped around, spraying each other with Gatorade and water, enjoying the moment together.

The celebration was short lived, however, as the Titans lost their next two district games, eliminating them from the postseason yet again. Coach War kept his behavior above the line, proving to Mr. Allen that he had indeed learned his lesson; he wanted to be defendable. Their final game was a total team win. They dominated their opponent at home, winning by three touchdowns to finish the season a much improved 6-3. In previous years, Coach War would have viewed the last game as meaningless, since there was no possible way the Titans could qualify for the playoffs. This year, however, was different. After his suspension, he appreciated his platform as a coach more and valued the relationships with his athletes. He vowed to send the seniors out on a winning note.

Sitting alone in the coaches' office after the game, Coach War heard his college coach again. "*You're either going in this direction, or you're going in this direction…*" He reflected on the successful season, raising his arm toward the ceiling. This year his team had a different trend line.

On Tuesday of the following week, Mitchell recognized the familiar piles of equipment strung throughout the locker room. Coach War was working to clean, fold, and store the Titans' gear before their mentoring session. He heard Mitchell coming down the hallway and smiled warmly when he entered the room. Coach War set his clipboard on the edge of his desk before reaching to shake Mitchell's hand.

"Coach," Mitchell said, extending his arm, "great season. I'm proud of the progress you made over the last year."

"Thanks," Coach War replied, "our kids worked hard. They earned success."

"No," Mitchell corrected, his voice light-hearted. "I don't know your kids, so I can't speak about them. I'm proud of the progress *you've* made over the last year."

Coach War beamed. He was so grateful to have Mitchell as his mentor.

"So, what's the plan for the offseason?" Mitchell asked, unzipping his light jacket as he walked toward his usual spot on the couch.

"Well, I'm really interested in hearing more about The Process of the 'Ship. I think your ideas on building meaningful relationships helped me capture the hearts of my athletes, and I know next year I can do more." Coach War leaned forward on the opposite couch, folding his hands, ready to listen intently. "I'm dying to know… what's the second phase of the process?"

"Yes," Mitchell agreed, "you made great strides with your team this season, and I am proud of the things you did to purposefully build relationships. I think you're ready for the second phase too, but before we get to that, let me ask you… how much do you read?"

Read? Coach War thought, wondering what that could have to do with improving his team. *Why does that matter? There's no way reading can end in 'ship. I teach PE not Language Arts.*

"Well, unless you count text messages, emails, or bedtime stories, I *don't* read."

Mitchell was not surprised.

"You need to. Coach, do you realize that if you read eight pages every day, just eight pages, you would accumulate nearly three thousand pages read by the end of the year? That's about one book a month. It might not seem like much, but one book a month, throughout a year, over the course of many years, can add a wealth of value to you as a person."

Coach War did the mental math. Mitchell's numbers added up, but he was perplexed as to how this could help him run a more successful football program.

"Most people can read eight pages in about ten minutes," Mitchell claimed.

"But what does this have to do with football?"

"It helps you sharpen your axe! Have you forgotten about the lumberjack?"

Coach War furrowed his eyebrows. Of course he hadn't. He thought about the lumberjack every day. He liked to start his day by visualizing the lumberjack swinging his axe over and over in his mind, slaving away in the forest, on his morning run.

"You see, reading will help you stay in the know with what others are doing. It will also give you ideas to try with your team. You can read anything. It doesn't matter if you are interested in fiction or nonfiction, business or sports… there is something valuable in everything. As long as you read eight pages a day, your axe will never get dull."

"But what does this have to do with The Process of the 'Ship?" Coach War's tone escalated from pushy to demanding. He desperately wanted to know Mitchell's secret formula.

"It's quite simple really," Mitchell explained. "While relationships are the process's foundation, the second phase is to build leadership into your team. And Coach," Mitchell emphasized, "leaders are readers!"

Knowing that Coach War was swamped, Mitchell cut their time short, rising off the couch. Even though Coach War now looked forward to their meetings, he appreciated Mitchell's thoughtfulness, giving up a few minutes so he could attend to his professional duties. Before he left the coaches' office, Mitchell reached into the side of his coat, pulling out a small book.

"I wanted to wait until the end of the season to give you this. I think you will find it helpful. Eight pages of reading, over the course of the next week, puts you on about page fifty by next Tuesday. I'm curious to see what you think."

Coach War extended his hand, accepting Mitchell's gift. He set the book on his desk, trading it for his clipboard so he could resume his team inventory. Holding the clipboard, Coach War stared at two hands wearing football gloves that spanned across the middle of the book's cover. The book's title was written in red letters above the hands, and Coach War read it to himself. Mitchell had given him *Culture Defeats Strategy* by Texas high school football coach and transformational leader Randy Jackson. Though he did not know it at the time, Mitchell's gift would change Titan Football forever.

Chapter Twenty-Six

"Tough People Win"

Coach War found reading every day easier than he anticipated. It fit naturally into his evening routine. Every night Mrs. Warrington would do the dishes in the kitchen, while he gave the kids baths, reading them a story before tucking them into bed. They would relax together when everything was done, nestling into the big black leather sectional that wrapped around their living room, watching one of the recorded shows on their DVR; *Shark Tank* was their favorite. When the Warringtons met at the end of the night on the couch, Mrs. Warrington cued up the latest episode.

"Not tonight," Coach War said. "You watch whatever you want, I have to read."

"You? Read? Since when?" Laura teased.

"Since now. Mitchell thinks this book will help me, so I'm going to give it a try. You know, he's been right about all the changes I made so far."

And so, from that night on, while his wife watched *Shark Tank,* he read his eight pages. He found himself looking forward to his reading time. By the following Tuesday, he was well past page fifty in the book.

Coach War thumbed through the pages he had read throughout the week while he waited for Mitchell. He jotted down some notes on his legal pad, highlighting his favorite parts and insights.

Mitchell was right on time, although moving noticeably slower than usual. He looked terrible. His face was puffy and red, and it wrinkled as he coughed. *Great, cold and flu season is coming early this year*, Coach War thought, having to help Mitchell sit down.

"Good to see you, Coach."

"You too, I guess. Are you OK?"

"Me? Oh, fine, just a little head cold, that's all."

Coach War scratched his head. Mitchell looked worse than simply having a little head cold. But he shrugged it off.

"So, how's the reading?"

"Great, actually. Thank you so much for this book. You were right… it *is* full of ideas."

Mitchell smiled.

"Coach, if you are going to integrate authentic leadership in your program, we need to design and establish a culture of leadership through your personal brand."

Coach War wasn't sure what he meant.

"What would you say is the brand of Titan Football?"

Again, he wasn't sure. He had never thought about his team's brand. Shrugging his shoulders, Coach War threw up his arms.

"And that's the problem!" Mitchell stated. "The brand of your program is your trademark. It should encompass everything your team stands for. It should be so clear that people not only know what it is, they should know what it looks like, what it sounds like, and most importantly, they need to *believe* in it. Coach Jackson's brand is very clear. Do you know what it is?"

"Tough people win?" Coach War guessed. He felt like a dart player hoping to hit the bulls-eye.

"Yes! Tough people win. It's everywhere in his program. It's on his players' shirts and in their locker room. It's even in his Twitter handle."

How does Mitchell know about Twitter? Coach War wondered.

"I'll ask you again, what is your program's brand? Could you tell me?"

"I guess I don't have one," Coach War concluded.

"Then that's what we need to work on next. Here is your assignment. For next week, reread chapters two and three. Sit down with your legal pad and list the things that are most important to the success of Titan Football. These will be your core values. Once you have defined them, we can build on them. I'm excited to see what you will come up with."

Chapter Twenty-Seven

"Titan Tough"

All week Coach War tried to identify his program's core values. He went back through game notes and scouting reports, looking for reoccurring themes, but nothing really stood out. Unsure what to do next, Coach War decided to ask his team. *If the culture of our program is going to change, then it will have to start with our current players.* He drafted a mass email that went out to every person on next season's roster. Attached in the email was a Google Form that consisted of one question: what word do you associate most with Titan Football?

Within minutes, players had already begun to submit answers, and by the end of the day most of the responses were in. Coach War combed through the results of the survey that night after dinner. As he aggregated the data, one word appeared over and over again—tough. Like Randy Jackson, Coach War was constantly preaching the importance of toughness to his players.

Why does toughness matter so much in football? Coach War wondered. He recalled a quote that had been the Titan Football mantra a few years ago… "Tough times don't last, but tough people do." He thought about how he pushed kids during conditioning at practice and how he was always able to squeeze just a little more out of a struggling athlete with the words "You're too tough to quit!" And then there was his dad's last advice before his first training camp in college.

"Son," his dad had said, sitting behind the wheel in the dorm parking lot, his left forearm casually resting on the driver-side window of the family SUV, "people do dumb things in college, so I'll just tell you that if you're going to be dumb, you'd better be tough."

Coach War remembered how he shook his dad's hand through the car door, then stood on the curb, waving goodbye as his parents drove away.

After reading the results, Coach War asked his wife what she thought. She agreed that toughness played a large part in succeeding in such a physical sport.

"That settles it," Coach War announced in their bedroom. "Our brand *has* to include toughness. Now, what phrase can I use to drive home the importance of toughness?"

The most powerful brands have a simple two-to-six-word phrase that sums up what an organization stands for. Laura turned out the light and nestled into bed. Coach War joined her, thinking of some of his favorite brands and their tag lines.

"Just Do It" from Nike. "Think Different" was Apple's. And "Eat Fresh" was Subway's.

And his personal favorite from President Donald Trump… "Make America Great Again."

Laura's voice pierced the veil of night.

"What about Titan toughness?" she offered to her husband. "You know, for your short tag line?"

"Not bad," Coach War affirmed, excited about the idea's merit. "But what if we shortened it to just Titan tough?"

"Titan tough," she repeated out loud. She rolled over in the bed to snuggle next to her husband. "It's simple, catchy, and easy to remember," she agreed. "I like it."

"From now on," Coach War told his wife, "we won't just be tough, we will be 'Titan Tough.'" And the program's brand was born.

Chapter Twenty-Eight

The Mirror Test

On Tuesday, Coach War told Mitchell about the "Titan Tough" tag line; Mitchell loved it.

"I think you nailed it, Coach."

Mitchell was even more impressed that Coach War had sought player input.

"Smart. When players have a voice," he buzzed with sing-song excitement, "they tend to have a greater level of buy-in. Are you still reading?" Mitchell asked.

"Every night. I'm about halfway through the book you gave me," Coach War confirmed.

"Good! Reading eight pages a day is easy to do, but it's also easy *not* to do. I'm glad to see you are being disciplined about it."

Coach War had never considered reading to be a form of self-discipline, but he liked Mitchell's perspective.

"Any 'aha' moments so far?"

Thumbing through the pages of the book, Coach War browsed through his highlights.

"I really like the 'You vs. Yesterday' concept."

"Why?" Mitchell asked, wanting Coach War to go deeper.

"It's about getting better all the time. You know, self-reflecting, seeing your current reality, then making the necessary changes to improve."

"Well, have you ever heard of the Mirror Test?"

Coach War shook his head.

"Every year I get a ton of graduation announcements. I make sure to give each graduate a handshake and a handwritten letter. My advice in every letter is to remember the Mirror Test. Every day, you need to look yourself in the mirror and ask the hard questions. Make peace with the decisions you've made and then focus on the areas you need to change. If you can look at yourself and be proud of who you are, you've passed the Mirror Test."

Coach War loved it. The Mirror Test was identical to the You vs. Yesterday self-reflection philosophy.

"Sounds like this could be one of your program's core values," Mitchell probed. "Think about a typical week in-season. Where might the Mirror Test fit into what you already do?"

Coach War thought about his typical week in-season.

"Mondays," he announced as if waking up out of a coma. "Mondays would be perfect! We start the week off by watching our game from the previous Friday night. It's like we are holding up a mirror for the players to evaluate themselves and our team's performance. As coaches, we use this opportunity to correct what we need to before our next game. Hudl is a digital mirror."

"It sounds logical then to assign the Mirror Test to your Monday routine."

"That's it," Coach War exclaimed. "Mirror Test Monday!"

And the Titans not only had their program's first core value, but had assigned it to a day of the week in the process.

Chapter Twenty-Nine

What it Means to Be "Titan Tough"

The Titans' in-season weekly routines continued to occupy Coach War's thoughts. Each day of the week held a specific purpose in preparing for Friday night. Mondays were about self-reflection, using video to correct mistakes and improve. Tuesday's focus was on installing the game plan. By Wednesday, the team needed to believe that victory was attainable, and on Thursday, the Titans had to trust that everybody understood their role in the game plan and were prepared to do their jobs. And on Friday, the hay was in the barn; it was time to execute. Every day counted. These weekly routines defined what it meant to be Titan Tough.

Coach War drew a rough chart on the top page of his legal pad. In the first column, he listed his program's five core values. Next, he aligned each core value to a day of the week, giving it a theme. Finally, Coach War created a hand gesture that players could use to remember each day's theme. When he had finished, he admired his work.

Core Value	Day of the Week and Theme	Hand Gesture
Self-Reflection	"Mirror Test" Monday	Hold your palm in front of your face as if you were holding a mirror.
Preparation	"Pack Your Own Parachute" Tuesday	Use both arms to mimic holding a rifle. Cock the imaginary gun with one pump down its barrel, as if preparing for war.
Belief	"Why Not?" Wednesday	Place your palms up at shoulder level along your sides, as if you were asking a question.
Trust	"Titan Trust" Thursday	Make a fist with your right hand. Move the fist across your body, tapping your heart twice.
Grit	Game Day Grit	Make a fist with either hand, then pound it against your opposite palm.

On Tuesday, Coach War showed Mitchell his rough weekly outline. Mitchell was immensely satisfied that Coach War was not only reading Randy Jackson's work, but using it as a model for his program.

"I love your team's core values, Coach. Taking the time to create your brand, identify your core values, and infuse them into the things your team already does has given you a clearer understanding of your team's purpose. Have you thought about taking your culture to the next level by creating a team language?"

"Create a language? What do you mean?"

Mitchell rummaged through his coaching bag.

"Are you familiar with the All Blacks?" he asked, pulling out another small book. He handed it to Coach War.

Coach War nodded his head emphatically, raising both eyebrows. How could he *not* know about the New Zealand All Blacks? They were the most successful professional organization in all of sports. From 2000 to 2009, the All Blacks boasted a winning percentage of over .800. During this era, one of Coach War's teammates at the University of Okoboji moved to New Zealand to continue to play football after college, teaching and growing the game on the island. All he talked about was the All Blacks, New Zealand's national rugby team. He would text Coach War videos of the pregame haka, the traditional war dance displaying an island tribe's strength, unity, and pride.

"Hell yeah," Coach War exclaimed. "The All Blacks are awesome. The haka gets me juiced every time I see it."

"Did you know that the All Blacks have their own language?"

Coach War shook his head. "I thought they just spoke English."

"No." Mitchell laughed. "They do, but they also have their own *team* language. Check out Chapter XII in this book, then ask yourself how this could be a model for your team."

Coach War accepted the little black book, reading its title and author to himself. Mitchell had given him a copy of *Legacy* by James Kerr.

"You might even already have your own language," Mitchell continued. "Do the players know what you are going to say *before* you say it?"

Coach War thought before responding.

"Well I do repeat myself a lot."

"See if you can come up with a short catch-phrase that fits each of your core values and themed days. Play around with the idea this week, and we can talk more about it next Tuesday." Mitchell winked at Coach War, rising off the couch to shake coach's hand. "I'm so proud of you," he affirmed. "Your hard work will really pay off. I promise you."

Chapter Thirty

Languages Start Revolutions

Mitchell was right… *Legacy* was a great read. Coach War especially liked the All Blacks mantras that were sprinkled throughout Chapter XII. With his nose buried in the book, he paced around his kitchen island. Laura unwrapped a package of popcorn for a late-night snack, laying it flat on the circular tray in the microwave; she started the timer as her husband read his favorite mantras aloud, pausing after each phrase for dramatic effect.

"No one is bigger than the team."

"It's not enough to be good. It's about being great."

"Leave it all out on the field."

"It's not the jersey. It's the man *in* the jersey."

"Once an All Black, always an All Black."

"Work harder than an ex-All Black."

Coach War was interrupted by the ding of the microwave timer. Laura opened the bag, emptying steaming hot popcorn into a large bowl. The smell of the fresh, buttery snack heightened Coach War's mood.

"So why don't you do that with your football team?" she encouraged. "Come on now, put down that book and relax. We have a new episode of *Shark Tank* to watch."

* * *

The next day during his prep, Coach War barricaded himself in the coaches' office. He stared at the top page of his legal pad, examining the chart he had recently created. He went down the list, beginning with Mirror Test Monday, trying to come up with a short catch-phrase.

The eye in the sky doesn't lie, he thought. That's definitely part of our team language.

But that was his phrase, not the players'.

Do the kids even know what that means, or am I flying B-52 bombers straight over their heads? He paused, letting his mind drift back to his playing days in college.

Friday afternoons in college football are light. Most teams use practice time for one final walk-through before the next day's game. Friday's dress at the University of Okoboji was helmets and grays—team-issued T-shirts and matching shorts. *The grays looked ridiculous*, Coach War remembered. Everyone's shirts were at least two sizes too big, while the shorts were ball-busters that resembled the NBA's Daisy Dukes of the eighties. *Why wasn't it the other way around?* he wondered. *The shorts should be two sizes too big and our T-shirts should be snug.*

Anyway, he told himself, shaking his head, letting his mind drift back to the Friday afternoons he experienced as a player. After the walk-through, the team had gathered around the goalpost in the north end zone. The coaches left the field, walking back to the athletic complex, respecting the players' tradition and privacy. Gazing out over Okoboji's West Lake, the players took a knee around their captains. Whitecap waves lapped against the rocks along the shore. When the coaches were out of ear-shot, "Goal Post" would begin. Nearly one hundred young men would utter a short phrase in unison.

"Yesterday's over, it's in our past. Let's look to Saturday and kick some ass!"

The guys would laugh, casting big belly grunts out to sea with the lake breeze. One of the captains would quiet the group down with a simple question.

"Who has poetry?"

Players looked forward to poems created by their teammates. No topic was off-limits. Poems commonly made fun of the coaches, the opponent, different position groups, or even a teammate who had done something embarrassing in the time since their last gathering. The unwritten rule of Goal Post was: the more crude the content, the better the poem. One poet at a time would make their way to the front of the semi-circle and stand against the white goalpost, ready to spit a few bars for the entertainment of their teammates.

If the poem was good, loud whooping could be heard all the way to the dorms on the other side of the lake. But, if the poem was not up to par, players would chastise the bard, hissing at him like the members of Delta House in the 1978 film *Animal House*. The crowd would throw Gatorade cups at their teammate, vocalizing their displeasure.

"That's it!" Coach War shouted, as if being struck by a lightning bolt. "It's edgy and provocative, and defendable *if* I tweak some of the words."

Uncapping a blue pen, Coach War wrote out the Goal Post phrase, stringing the words across the header. He quickly made a few changes. "Yesterday," was replaced with "Friday," and "Saturday" became "game day." Coach War rehearsed his revised work out loud in a soft voice.

"Friday night's over, it's in our past. Let's look to game day and kick some ass!"

He knew the Titans would *love* saying this last part, but he saw an opportunity to make it part of his team's language. He crossed out "and kick some ass," inserting another short phrase in its place. He read his modifications aloud again; this time his voice was stronger.

"Friday night's over, it's in our past. Let's look to game day and sharpen our axe!"

Perfect! He now had a catch-phrase for Monday that aligned to its theme and core value. The bell rang before he could move on to Tuesday. *It'll have to wait.* Coach War smiled as he walked toward the gym. He had momentum, and he could feel his team culture continue to move forward. Above the chart, he named his language. From now on, his team would not just speak English, they would be fluent in Titanic.

Chapter Thirty-One

Titanic

Coming up with Titanic, the language of Titan Football, was easier than expected. Now that Monday's phrase was done, Coach War's creative juices brewed as he worked to create a catch-phrase for the other days of the week. Thinking about "Pack Your Own Parachute Tuesday," Coach War closed his eyes, imagining himself in the grainy black and white paratrooper footage.

The cargo hold of the airplane was dark. The only visible light was a small red dot above the hatch. Coach War sat on a long, steel bench; it was cold. His hair itched inside the webbing of the hard helmet, which slid from side to side with any sudden movement. His eyes were wide, fixed on the jumpmaster who was standing in a flight suit to the right of the closed hatch near the red light. The officer's right arm was fully extended, gripping the hatch handle; his left arm was bent at a ninety-degree angle so that his eyes could see his watch. The light just above the jumpmaster's head illuminated his face, allowing Coach War to see him mouth the seconds as they passed. He counted down from ten once the airplane entered the jump zone. When he reached zero, the jumpmaster twisted his hips, springing open the hatch, exposing the soldiers to the gaping atmosphere.

"Get some, boys, it's go time. Lock and load!" the jumpmaster ordered.

Coach War's eyes popped open. *Bingo*. Lock and load suited Pack Your Own Parachute Tuesday and became the week's second catch-phrase.

Wednesday practices had a tendency to drag; "Hump Day" was the most mundane day of the week in the Titans' preparation routine. While the coaches knew that game day was just around the corner, to a high school student, Friday night seemed about as close as Mars. The Titans conditioned *and* lifted on Wednesdays, pushing the athletes to exhaustion. This was the dirty work of preparing to win. Wednesday was the day of the week the players complained about the most. Coach War saw his Titanic as an opportunity to change his team's mid-week mindset.

"Why Not? Wednesday" was both the daily theme and catch-phrase. What if on Wednesdays the players could only respond by saying "Why not?" to anything asked of them? Coach War dreamt about the possibilities.

Run another sprint, the coaches could demand.

"Why not?"

Do auxiliary lifts along with the core lifts.

"Why not?"

Attend a mandatory team study table.

"Why not?"

Coach War smiled. This could provide the extra lift his players needed to surge into game day. He moved on to Thursday.

Thursday was all about trust. Coaches had to trust the game plan they had devised and installed throughout the week, trusting that they had put their team in a position to be successful on game day. Players, on the other hand, had to be able to trust their coaches and commit to the game plan; after all, they would be the ones responsible for its execution. "Play the Game Thursday" gave Coach War a chance to evaluate how well his players trusted that week's game plan and each other.

Off the field, trust was needed to take Titan Talk to a more meaningful level. Coach War was already planning the second installment of Titan Talk, making it more rigorous with prompts like:

"When you make a mistake, what do you tell yourself to move on to the next play?" and "Who is a hero in your life? What makes this person admirable?" These questions would take the athlete on a journey inside themselves, the way that Mitchell had done with him. Trust was vital because sharing meant players would have to take a risk. Players who shared during Titan Talk would be exposing themselves to criticism and ridicule from those around them. *Players will only open up if they can trust one another*, Coach War concluded. *A greater level of trust means a deeper conversation.*

Coach War reflected on how he would define trust for his team. Trust was not something you said, it had to be felt. Trust had to be authentic. Trust was knowing that your teammate would not let you down. And then it hit him. In the game of football, regular trust didn't cut it. If his team was going to win, they needed to have "Titan Trust." The standard for measuring Titan Trust depended on how you answered one simple question: would I get in a foxhole with you? If your answer was yes, then that was a teammate you could count on. You knew that they had your back. Getting in a foxhole with someone required more than trust; it required Titan Trust.

Coach War brainstormed several war analogies that he could use to go along with the foxhole test that would serve as the short phrase for Titan Trust. In the end, however, he opted for clear communication. *When the game's on the line, I don't want kids to mince words, wondering what to say. I just want them to do their job.* He decided that the only way to prove you would climb into a foxhole with a teammate was to look that person in the eye and say, "I trust you."

On game day, however, no catch-phrase was necessary; the pads did the talking. Players would speak Titanic by being gritty and Titan Tough. Reading over his notes, he smiled. He couldn't wait to show Mitchell.

Chapter Thirty-Two

"Who Am I? I Am A Titan."

That night Coach War thought about the core values that would make his players "Titan Tough." Sinking into his leather sectional, he scribbled around the chart on his legal pad. He wanted to create a players' creed that encompassed everything his program was about. *Creeds call people toward a cause. Repetition drives home their message. They are memorable.*

Laura cued up a murder mystery on the DVR, while Coach War continued to doodle on his note pad. He closed his eyes, visualizing Dr. Martin Luther King, Jr. giving his "I Have a Dream" speech in front of the Lincoln Memorial. *Now that's a creed,* he said to himself, thinking about Dr. King's legacy. "We aren't at the top of the mountain yet, but look at the progress that's been made in the last fifty years."

He reopened his eyes, remembering a YouTube video that Coach Roman had shared with the football staff before the Lone Tree game last season. In the video, a high school football coach is addressing his team before a game. Dashing off the couch, Coach War retrieved his iPhone from the kitchen counter. Combing through his school inbox, he found the email that contained the link to the video. Leaning on the kitchen island, he clicked the link. As the video loaded, Coach War went back to the sectional to grab his legal pad, flipping it open to a new page. He watched the coach speak, restarting the video again and again, absorbing the coach's message to his team.

Over and over he heard, "Who am I? I am a champion." Coach War's mind raced. He frantically scribbled "I Am A Champion" on the top of the fresh page. He crossed out champion, replacing it with Titan. Coach War's creed would begin with "I Am A Titan." Beneath the title of his creed, Coach War described the five core values of Titan Football, along with a short definition of what each meant. When he was done, he reread it aloud.

"Who Am I? I Am A Titan."

> I am a Titan. My team is my mirror. Every day I will look into the mirror and choose to get 1 percent better than I was yesterday. Who am I? I am a Titan. I promise to Pack My Own Parachute. I will take responsibility for the things that I can control, and I will be prepared to answer the call when my time comes. My parachute is locked and loaded. I will not let the team down. Who am I? I am a Titan. I speak fluent Titanic and will not undermine or sabotage the culture of Titan Football. I will selflessly serve the team. Together Everyone Achieves More, and we can accomplish *anything*. Who am I? I am a Titan. I trust my teammates and coaches. I believe that the coaches care about me as a person and will help me succeed. I trust the game plan and will execute it to the best of my abilities, no matter what my role is on the team. I trust my teammates to do their jobs so the team will earn success. Who am I? I am a Titan. I am relentless. My grit will not let me quit. I will face all challenges and strive to overcome them. Who am I? I am a Titan, and I am Titan Tough.

Chapter Thirty-Three

The "Titan Tough" MVP

Coach War had a hard time keeping all the new pieces of the Titan Football program straight. The more he added, the more they ran together in his mind. He had notes on everything, but with core values, hand gestures, a new language to learn, and now a creed, it was impossible to keep track of. *If I can't keep it all straight, how can the kids?* Coach War thought. His legal pad had become a dumping ground for notes, and it felt disorganized and chaotic.

That night, while Laura caught up on *This Is Us*, he opened his Google Drive and began working on a document that would serve as a master blueprint to the program's culture, something he decided to call the "Titan Tough" MVP. Coach War re-created the chart from his legal pad on the document, adding his team's mission and vision to the program's principles, his MVP, along with the creed. The team mission combined the first two phases from Mitchell's The Process of the 'Ship. The vision was the hope that every athlete would become Titan Tough, and the team motto for next year was obvious: "Sharpen the Axe." Coach War was surprised at how quickly he organized his ideas. When he was finished, he showed it to his wife.

"Looks like you've invested a lot of time in your team," she said, impressed with his new document. "I don't really understand it, but I hope it helps you win more next fall."

Coach War hoped so too, although he knew that winning was irrelevant by now. He sat next to his wife on the living room sectional. Admiring his work one more time, he took pride in the product that had all started with Mitchell and a single question: Why do I coach?

On Tuesday, Coach War handed Mitchell the "Titan Tough" MVP, which he had printed on blue cardstock. His right leg bounced wildly as Mitchell looked it over.

The "Titan Tough" MVP			
MISSION	To build relationships and leadership in young adults so they will grow into men of character.		
VISION	Every Titan football player will be "Titan Tough," physically and mentally.		
MOTTO	"SHARPEN THE AXE!"		
CORE VALUES:	**Theme of the Week**	**Hand Gesture**	**Titanic**
Self-Reflection	Mirror Test Monday	Hold out your hand as if looking in a mirror.	"Friday night's over, it's in our past. Let's look to Game Day and sharpen our axe!"
Preparedness	Pack Your Own Parachute Tuesday	Use both arms to mimic holding a rifle. Cock the imaginary gun with one pump down its barrel.	"Lock and load!"
Belief	Why Not? Wednesday	Place your palms up at shoulder level along your sides, as if you were asking a question.	"Why not?!"
Trust	"Titan Trust" Thursday	Make a fist with your right hand. Move the fist across your body, tapping your heart twice.	"I trust you."
Grit	Game Day Grit	Make a fist with either hand, then pound it against your opposite palm.	Let the pads do the talking.
"TITAN TOUGH" CREED	I am a Titan. My team is my mirror. Every day I will look into the mirror and choose to get 1% better than I was yesterday. Who am I? I am a Titan. I promise to Pack My Own Parachute. I will take responsibility for the things that I can control, and I will be prepared to answer the call when my time comes. My parachute is locked and loaded; I will not let the team down. Who am I? I am a Titan. I speak fluent Titanic and will not undermine or sabotage the culture of Titan Football. I will selflessly serve the team. Together Everyone Achieves More and we can accomplish *anything*. Who am I? I am a Titan. I trust my teammates and coaches. I believe that the coaches care about me as a person and will help me succeed. I trust the game plan and will execute it to the best of my abilities, no matter what my role is on the team. I trust my teammates to do their jobs, so the team will earn success. Who am I? I am a Titan. I am relentless. My grit will not let me quit. I will face all challenges and strive to overcome them. Who am I? I am a Titan, and I am "Titan Tough."		

"Very impressive," Mitchell said, grinning from ear to ear. "It's easy to read, and the message is clear and very organized. Anyone who sees this would easily be able to understand what your program is about. This looks amazing."

Coach War beamed.

"Well done."

Coach War had invested hours in his team's culture and was excited to introduce the "Titan Tough" MVP to the team during fall camp.

An easy conversation went back and forth between Mitchell and Coach War over the course of the next hour. When the bell rang, forcing Coach War to teach his next class, Mitchell remained on the coaches' office couch. He stared at the "Titan Tough" MVP, unable to believe this was the same coach who had told his players they should commit to getting bigger, stronger, and faster or they might as well quit.

Chapter Thirty-Four

Seventeen Inches of Leadership

Coach War beat Mitchell to ChapaChino after leaving school the next Tuesday. It was opening day in Major League Baseball and, as lifelong Cubs fans, they had agreed to watch the opening day ceremonies at Wrigley Field together. Coach War taught in the morning but used half of a personal day to celebrate the occasion with Mitchell. He nervously watched the clock tick past one p.m.; the first pitch was scheduled for 1:20 CST. *He's never late,* Coach War thought, wondering if something had happened to Mitchell on his commute. Other excuses flashed through his mind. *Did he forget?* Coach War considered it briefly but dismissed that thought. *Nah, Mitchell never forgets.*

Another minute passed, then another. He had a server change the channel from daytime TV to WGN for the broadcast. Black and white highlights from previous opening days at the "Friendly Confines" reeled across the screen. Coach War watched the screen but continued to worry. At 1:13 p.m. the jingling of a tiny bell atop the entry door caught his ear. He looked up to see the coffee shop door swing inward as a man wearing a blue ball cap walked in. Mitchell had on his team-issue Cubs hat and was struggling to move. His black coaching bag kept snagging on anything in its path. Mitchell had to turn his hips sideways to prevent getting stuck in the doorway. When he had managed to squeeze through, Mitchell took a second to regain his composure. He spotted Coach War at their usual booth in the corner, maneuvering through the crowd toward the table.

What the hell is he wearing? Coach War wondered, noticing a ridiculously large object hanging around Mitchell's neck. It was black and looked heavy and awkward.

Mitchell was out of breath when he reached the booth. Coach War eyed the bulky rubber object Mitchell was wearing, sweat pouring down his face.

"Sorry I'm late," Mitchell apologized, sitting down. "I couldn't find my 'Opening Day' outfit." He winked. "All joking aside, thanks for meeting me here today to watch the game. I want to commend you for the work you have done. Your axe is sharper now than it ever has been. I'm so proud of you for taking the time and energy to become a better leader."

Coach War smiled.

"You are deep into the second phase of The Process of the 'Ship personally," Mitchell continued, "but now we need to bring leadership to your team."

"Is that why you're wearing that *thing?*" Coach War asked.

"It's hard to explain, so I thought I'd demonstrate."

Coach War was perplexed. *Demonstrate what? How to kill yourself?* Mitchell looked ridiculous.

Mitchell looked down, then struggled to turn the object hanging on the string around. He fought the material as it rubbed between his belly and the edge of the table. The black object became a white face, which Coach War immediately recognized. Mitchell was wearing a home plate from a little kid's playset.

"Coach, in honor of 'Opening Day,' how 'bout a little trivia. Do you know how big home plate is in Little League?"

Thinking for a moment, Coach War responded. "No, not a clue."

"Seventeen inches," Mitchell replied. "And how about in high school?"

Coach War took the bait. "Seventeen inches?" he guessed.

"Right!" Mitchell confirmed. "Now what about at TD Ameritrade in Omaha, the home of the College World Series?"

"Has to be seventeen inches," said a more confident Coach War with a smirk.

"Yes! Nailed it. And how big is home plate in the minors?"

Coach War knew the answer.

"Seventeen inches."

"But what about in Major League Baseball?"

"Again, seventeen inches." Coach War found this exchange interesting, but he wondered where Mitchell was going.

"Good. At every level of baseball, home plate is exactly seventeen inches wide," Mitchell explained. "The pinnacle of the pentagon forms from straight lines that are eight and a half inches long on each side. This point is comprised of two, twelve-inch long lines that create an apex when they intersect. The base of home plate is *always* seventeen inches."

Coach War had to grin at the crazy genius of Mitchell as he sat there with home plate dangling on his chest.

"Now," Mitchell continued, getting to the heart of the lesson, "what do they do with a big-league pitcher who can't throw over this seventeen-inch area?"

Coach War laughed, "Toss his ass out! Go to the bullpen!" He tapped his left hand against his right wrist three times, the universal gesture to bring out another hurler.

"Ah, yes! But, you know what they *don't* do?"

Coach War furled his eyebrows as Mitchell had again commanded his full attention.

"They don't say, 'hey, he's struggling, that's OK. So you can't find the seventeen-inch plate. We'll bring in an eighteen-inch plate. And if you can't hit that, we'll get a nineteen-inch plate, or even a twenty-inch plate. Surely you could throw strikes then.'"

"OK," Coach War said, trying to understand. "But what does this have to do with leadership and culture?"

"Without player leadership," Mitchell connected, "we are bringing in a wider plate. Every time someone shows up late to practice, fails a class, gets caught drinking at a party, is flagged fifteen yards for a personal foul, do you hold them accountable for their behavior, or do you make a personal ruling based on your emotions, putting your own interests above the team? In other words, do you widen the plate?"

Now Coach War saw where Mitchell was going. This was a lesson on the importance of a consistent personal standard. Mitchell held each side of the plate, struggling again to flip it between his belly and the table. Coach War fixated on the black rubber underside of the plate. Mitchell retrieved a black Sharpie from his coaching bag; its felt tip squeaked against the white top. Coach War watched Mitchell in bewilderment as he frantically scribbled. When Mitchell was done, he placed the cap back on the marker, setting it on the table. Again, Mitchell struggled to turn the plate to face Coach War, but this time he spun it upside down so the apex pointed up. Coach War stared at what looked like two small windows and a front door.

"This is the problem leaders are up against today," Mitchell explained. "Our homes, our families, our marriages, and the way we discipline. Kids know about accountability, but society keeps changing the rules. When they fail to meet the standards, we widen the plate!"

Coach War thought about his own parenting style. He found himself falling into the trap of threatening consequences all the time. His favorites were: "If you do that, then…" Or, "You'd better stop, or *else*." Or even, "I'm warning you…"

But he rarely followed through on the consequences when his kids crossed the line. His mind shifted to his football team. Home plate was even wider at school.

"Coach," Mitchell empathized, "it's not your fault. Our schools have been stripped of the tools they need in order to correct behavior and hold kids to a higher personal standard."

Coach War thought about how education had changed even throughout his short career. *It's no secret that the American family is falling apart, placing more and more responsibility on me as a teacher.*

"Increases in class size hamper teachers' ability to address inappropriate behavior," Mitchell rationalized. "Emphasis on student achievement, mainly standardized test scores, has widened the plate also."

Mitchell was preaching to the choir; Coach War had seen this happen time and time again.

"But this isn't just happening in our schools," Mitchell continued. "Our religious organizations and churches widen the plate too. Powerful people in positions of authority are taking advantage of young children. And what happens when their devious acts are discovered? Nothing. The incidents are swept under the rug and forgotten about. Our plate has widened."

Coach War sat in silence.

"Coach, the bottom line is that if you want to keep the home plate of Titan Football the standard size of seventeen inches, then you need to create a leadership council."

"What does a seventeen-inch plate have to do with a leadership council?" Coach War asked.

Mitchell smiled.

"How many players do you have on your team in a typical year? About one hundred?"

"Yes, a little less, but one hundred is a nice round number."

"Good. That means that every player is deserving of 1 percent of your time and energy. No more, no less. Is 1 percent fair?"

"I guess that's fair…" Coach War reasoned, his voice trailing off.

"There's no way you give each player 1 percent of your time and energy currently! You've widened the plate for some—those you give more than 1 percent of your time to—and you've shrunk the plate for others. A leadership council will help you keep the standard plate at seventeen inches." Mitchell pulled out another book from his coaching bag, extending it across the booth. Lifting the book to an eighty-degree angle, Coach War noticed Ohio State Head Coach Urban Meyer on the cover. He read the title to himself as Mitchell held it out. *Above The Line*.

"I want you to read Chapter Eight by next week. Urban Meyer writes about what he calls the '10-80-10 Principle.' The subtitle to this chapter is 'How to Build an Elite Team,' which is what you are trying to do for next year. Coach Meyer has won three NCAA championships and has some great ideas you could use with your players. Remember,

Coach, this…" Mitchell said, tapping the top of the house with his index finger, "…this is a mess. It is more important than ever that you teach kids to have a high personal standard. You need to define and model that standard, and, if you want to have an elite team, let the other players hold each other accountable."

Coach War thought about a quote from one of his favorite current coaches, P.J. Fleck. "Bad teams, no one leads. Average teams, coaches lead. But elite teams, players lead." Coach War desperately wanted to be part of an elite team. He could not wait to go home and dive into *Above the Line*. For the next few hours, they sat at ChapaChino talking and enjoying the ballgame. The Cubs beat the Brewers 4-1, and Coach War hummed "Go Cubs Go" as he walked to his car, swinging Mitchell's book in his right hand.

Chapter Thirty-Five

10-80-10 Principle

That night Coach War read beyond eight pages, leafing through Urban Meyer's book while his wife watched another show on the DVR after their kids were in bed. By now, Laura had adjusted to her husband's new habit, and she had gotten used to watching TV alone. Coach War flipped to chapter eight, wanting to dive right into the "10-80-10 Principle."

Urban Meyer used a giant circle to represent all of the people in any organization. Inside the outer-most circle were two subsequent circles. The smallest circle was located in the center of the organization and represented its nucleus. Another circle was just inside the edge of the organization's outer circle. Coach War put down the book; it stood as if it were a small tent on its pages, rising off the leather sectional seat. Running to the counter, Coach War found his trusty legal pad. He turned to the closest blank page to the front, labeling the top "Titan Football."

Drawing a small circle in the center of the page, Coach War began by focusing on the nucleus. Sitting back on the couch, he resumed reading. An organization's nucleus should consist of its top performers, representing 10 percent of the total population. The top ten-percenters are elite; they drive the decisions and culture of an organization giving all they have, all the time. To a top ten-percenter, work is not just their job, it is their calling. These people take initiative, are self-disciplined, selflessly serve others in the organization, and seek constant improvement. They are self-motivated and do not need anyone to push them. Coach War paused to reflect on some of Titan Football's top performers in recent years; these were the people he loved to coach. Inside the small circle, Coach War labeled his nucleus "True Titans."

The majority of the people in an organization comprise 80 percent of the population; this group is represented by the biggest circle, beginning directly outside of the nucleus. These individuals come to work every day, can be counted on to do their jobs, and respect their co-workers. The majority comply with authority and are committed to the organization but may not have the drive that the top ten-percenters in the nucleus do.

Coach War labeled the middle circle "The Majority."

The final circle was a thin band that extended around the peripheral of an organization, another group of 10-percenters, opposite of the nucleus. These ten-percenters are not committed to their work and are uninterested in helping the organization achieve its goals. In short, they coast, often doing the bare minimum. The peripheral ten-percenters fail to reach their potential, wasting whatever natural talent they may have had.

Coach War nodded along as he read, agreeing with Urban Meyer's synopsis of the last group of people. "*They are coach killers*." He highlighted those four words in the book, then set it on the seat next to him, trading the book for his legal pad. In the margin of the page along the outside circle, Coach War labeled this group "Coach Killers."

Coach War stared at his diagram, reflecting on how true the 10-80-10 Principle was. His mind jumped to an interview he saw last season on ESPN's *College Gameday*. Alabama was number one in the country at the time, and Nick Saban was preparing his team for a big game that week. In the interview, Coach Saban generalized that "mediocre people don't like high achievers, and high achievers don't like mediocre people."

Coach War zeroed in on his team's high achievers. *The nucleus of our team should be our leadership council*, he speculated. In the margins of the page next to his diagram, Coach War sketched out the basic criteria for his team's leadership council, his "True Titans," the team's nucleus.

1. Ten percent of our team is about ten players. Our leadership council will consist of ten members.
2. All four grade levels of the high school program will have representation. The leadership council will consist of three seniors, three juniors, two sophomores, and two freshmen.
3. Teammates will vote on the True Titans they want to represent their class. The highest vote-getters will be asked to join the leadership council.
4. True Titans will have a say in all areas of the program, including discipline. A leadership council vote will settle any issue that may arise.

Coach War set his pen down, picking the book back up to continue reading. "The leadership challenge is to move as many of the eighty-percenters into the nucleus as you can. If you can expand the top 10 percent into 15 percent or 20 percent, you are going to see a measurable increase in the performance of your team." Coach War marked his spot and closed his book. He stared at the TV, letting his mind wander. He imagined his True Titans leading, modeling for others what a Titan football player should be.

Coach War's mind shifted to the work that would be required to get a leadership council off the ground; it would not be easy. Then he envisioned his team's nucleus growing every day as a result of his purposeful planning and effort. He pictured the lumberjack standing at the grindstone in the early morning light, moving his axe blade back and forth meticulously, bright sparks flying across a workbench inside a small tool shed. *The work I do today will make my job easier in the future,* Coach War concluded. *I will never fully implement the second phase of The Process of The 'Ship if I don't commit to building player leadership.*

Chapter Thirty-Six

"True Titans"

On Friday, Coach War scheduled a five minute team meeting after school in the cafeteria where he would explain the leadership council and the purpose for its establishment. He spent his prep that day pacing in the coaches' office, where he timed himself as he rehearsed his spiel. If he could not explain the concept in five minutes or less, then he did not understand it well enough.

Coach War also composed three Google Forms, one for each grade level, beginning with the juniors, who were next season's seniors. Every player was listed alphabetically on their respective Google Form. Each player was asked to vote for individuals they would like to represent their grade by checking the box next to that player's name. The highest vote-getters would win the nomination and be invited to become a "True Titan." Anyone unwilling to serve on the leadership council could forfeit the position, and the next highest vote-getter would become eligible. Just for fun, Coach War penciled out who he would vote for if he was a player on a small piece of scratch paper. He tucked his secret vote into the cardboard spine of his legal pad.

A group of players beat Coach War to the cafeteria after school. When the room was full, Coach War spoke, first thanking them for their time, then outlining the ideology of the leadership council.

"I can't tell you exactly what your role as a True Titan will be yet," Coach War stated earnestly, "but I can guarantee that *you* will be *leading*."

Rumbling echoed across the cafeteria as players turned to one another, sharing their initial reaction to Coach War's news. He held out his hand, quieting his team down before explaining further.

"As a True Titan, you will be responsible for leading a summer lifting team. You will facilitate a small group during Titan Talk. And you will help hold your teammates accountable for their behavior if disciplinary action is warranted."

Again, the players turned toward one another to discuss Coach War's proposal.

"I'm emailing you a Google Form right after this meeting. You need to make your selections by Monday at eight a.m. Any questions?" he asked, pausing momentarily to scan the room. There were none; his message had been crystal clear. He looked at his watch; he had been speaking for just under four minutes.

"OK then. Dismissed. Have a great weekend."

The players stood, slinging their backpacks over their shoulders. The hallways buzzed with excitement as kids exited the cafeteria; many were talking about the possibility of becoming a True Titan.

Just as he said he would, Coach War sent out the Google Form immediately following the meeting. By Sunday night, nearly all the player responses had been submitted. Coach War looked over the aggregated data. While Laura watched TV, Coach War dislodged his True Titan predictions from the cardboard binding on the back of his legal pad. His eyes toggled between his computer screen and the small slip of paper as he compared the results to his prediction. The kids who he and the other coaches viewed as team leaders won by large margins of victory, becoming Coach War's inaugural True Titans. *Clearly the players understand who the most qualified leaders are on our team—why didn't I recognize it and trust them to lead before?*

Chapter Thirty-Seven

Handwritten Notes

Mitchell continued to spend Tuesday afternoons with Coach War, but his visits became less frequent. Coach War did not think much of it; it was May, and an increase in temperatures also brought an increase in activities. Besides, he was busy closing out another school year and preparing for summer training. A noticeable pile of graduation announcements began to occupy Coach War's desk. Kids would see him in the hall or stop by the gym to hand him a graduation announcement and invitation to their party.

Coach War was apathetic toward high school graduation. He was guaranteed to be invited to his players' parties, and he made it a point to go and sign the guest book. He might even enjoy a slice of cake. Staring at the pile that was accumulating on the corner of his desk, he questioned graduation etiquette. *Am I really expected to give a gift to* every *senior who invites me to their party?* A congratulatory handshake was the only gift he ever handed out. After all, he had always believed that his time over the last four years was each graduate's gift.

On Tuesday of the seniors' last week, he was sitting at his desk mindlessly turning his latest graduation announcement over in his hands. Mitchell interrupted Coach War's daydream with a knock on the brick wall.

"Heelllooooo…" he announced, stepping into his office.

Coach War blinked his eyes, snapping to life. He rose out of his chair, extending his hand toward Mitchell. The two walked toward their usual places in the coaches' office. Mitchell let out a barking cough as he sat down.

"You still have that cough?" Coach War asked.

"Oh, I guess winter doesn't want to go away."

Coach realized Mitchell didn't want to talk about it but wondered if there was more to it than just a cough.

Mitchell quickly changed the subject. "What's that in your hand?"

"Oh, this," Coach War said, surprised. "Just another graduation announcement for the pile on my desk." He tapped the card twice against his leg. "Say, Mitchell, did you go to graduation parties when you were teaching?"

"Still do," Mitchell said, perking up. "My wife and I love them. We go to every single one we are invited to. Such a great time in a teenager's life, don't you think?"

A dreamy smile swept across Mitchell's face.

"I guess, but do you give a gift to *every* graduate?" Coach War asked.

"I *do*," Mitchell confirmed.

"But doesn't that get, you know, expensive?"

"Well," Mitchell said, "my standard gift doesn't cost much. Just time and a little effort."

Coach War tilted his head. "What do you mean?"

"Coach, my gift is never monetary. That *would* get expensive."

"So what do you give?"

"Every graduate receives a handshake and a handwritten note."

Coach War was confused. "Like a card?"

"No, a handwritten note, usually written on festive stationery."

"And what do you say, just congratulations?"

"Oh yes, congratulations is in there, but that's only how I begin and conclude the letter. I usually share a memory of each student, then offer a piece of advice for the future. Handwritten notes can be very powerful, don't you think?"

Coach War thought back to the time before his own high school graduation. After his senior football season, he began receiving quite a bit of attention from college recruiters hoping he would continue to play ball at their universities. No one from division one schools ever called, but there was lots of interest from smaller local schools offering modest scholarships. Coach War remembered how he did not enjoy the recruiting process. His dad, on the other hand, did, and, true to his blue-collar roots, ranked each school's interest in Vinny according to the dollars they were offering. The school offering the most money became the front-runner.

Vinny was undecided on his next move until after Christmas when the University of Okoboji came calling. Situated in Milford, Iowa, Okoboji was a short, two-hour drive from his hometown. The proximity meant his parents could make every home game. On his official visit, eighteen-year-old Vinny marveled at the bottomless blue water of West Lake Okoboji and was told story after story about the wild summer weekends that lake life brought. He was already hooked when he met the football coach, Jerry Heartwell.

Coach Heartwell was a winner. Five consecutive conference titles resulting in playoff appearances made the thought of playing college football appealing. Coach Heartwell won over Mr. Warrington when he mentioned that his dad was a coal miner from rural West Virginia. The scholarship money did not matter to Mr. Warrington after that. But above all, Coach Heartwell was authentic. Every week after his official visit, all the way up to National Signing Day, Vinny received a handwritten note that began with the words: "From The Desk Of Coach Jerry Heartwell…" While the other schools sent fancy letters with generic words typed across an emblazoned foil letterhead, Coach Heartwell's letters were personal, and his handwriting was unmistakable. He wrote in all caps, a thick blue felt tip ink pen forming each large, blocky letter. His words were simple, but from the heart.

Mom and Dad still have all those letters saved, I bet, Coach War thought as he listened to Mitchell describe his high school graduation tradition. *Yes, handwritten notes are powerful indeed.*

Coach War frantically scribbled out Mitchell's graduation letter outline on his way out of the Coaches' office. *How did it go again? Oh yes. Congratulations. Memory. Advice for the future.*

"Got it!" he exclaimed, power walking to the gym to avoid being tardy for his next class.

Chapter Thirty-Eight

"You'll Never Be Broke"

Mrs. Warrington came home with the kids after work and found Coach rummaging through the party supplies stored in a tote in the basement. Hats, streamers, and every decoration known to man illustrated where he had been, strung out in a trail behind him.

"What do you think you are doing?" she inquired.

Coach War slowly turned toward his wife, away from his mess, noticing how she was tapping her left foot. The black stiletto heel that matched her pinstripe business suit clicked like an assault rifle against the basement's concrete floor. Her hands rested firmly on each hip; Coach War knew he was in trouble.

"Ummm…," he pleaded. "Looking for the scrapbook paper."

Laura pointed him toward another tote in the opposite corner of the room. She continued to tap her foot furiously as he read the side of the tote, which was labeled "Scrapbook Paper" in big black Sharpie letters. He smiled nervously, moving toward the tote he had been looking for.

"And, honey," she scolded as if talking to their oldest daughter, "don't come upstairs until this mess has been picked up!"

She pivoted on the long stem of her heel, left the room and climbed the stairs. When she was safely out of earshot, Coach War soured his face, moving his head from side to side as he mocked her.

"I heard that!" she bellowed down the stairs.

* * *

That night, Coach War didn't read. Instead, he sat at the dining room table with a piece of scrapbook paper and wrote out his first graduation letter. He wrote another one, then another, finding his stride. He put each letter in a large manila envelope before checking the graduate's name off his list. Coach War's favorite part of the letter was the closing. Taping a one-dollar bill to the bottom of the page, Coach War offered his life advice: "As long as you have this letter, you'll never be broke." Then just above his signature was a signature phrase. "Titans always finish on top! I'm proud of you."

Actually, Coach War was proud of himself. Mitchell's outlook on graduation inspired him to do more, and again he made a choice to act. There was solace in writing, and he hoped that at least one of his letters would comfort a student during a time of need or uncertainty in adulthood. He went to bed with a greater level of peace than he had experienced in a long time. As he lay in bed, the still darkness of the evening engulfing his body, a vision of the lumberjack standing next to a pile of wood lingered in the subconscious of his mind. Wearing a red flannel shirt and a smile the size of Lake Michigan, the lumberjack stood, admiring the fruits of his labor. His razor-sharp axe glistened in the early evening sunlight as it leaned against the cords of freshly cut timber. Coach War closed his eyes, knowing that he was now cutting down more trees than he ever had before.

Chapter Thirty-Nine

Draft Day

The inaugural group of True Titans, minus the freshmen who would join the council in the fall, met for the first time on Saturday afternoon at Coach War's house. Eight athletes lounged in the early summer sun on his deck, relaxing on his patio furniture, sipping Gatorade and enjoying each other's company. Coach War manned the grill, wearing sunglasses, flip-flops, shorts, and a Titan Football T-shirt. He dished out burgers and hot dogs while his kids ran around, entertaining the high school students with stunts on the backyard playground. It was a picture-perfect day. The conversation was light, centering on the end of school and graduation parties they planned on attending. Two sophomores bragged about having Kendrick Lamar tickets for Sunday night in Omaha. They were taking their girlfriends, and the other guys were envious.

After everyone had eaten, Laura slid open the glass doors connecting their deck to the kitchen.

"Maya, Ella," she called. "Time to come in!"

The kids pretended not to hear their mom, continuing to play amid Coach War's players. She stormed off the deck, stomping down to the playground. She scooped Ella up, holding her tightly as she lugged her middle child away so Coach War could get the meeting started. The players laughed as they witnessed the scene.

"Dang, dude!" Remmy clowned with a teammate. "Did you see that?"

Coach War responded to Remmy's comment.

"Mrs. Warrington doesn't play around!"

The deck broke out in laughter.

"Gentlemen," he continued, refocusing his players' attention, "it's draft day."

The players cheered.

Coach War used his kids' whiteboard easel to make a chart. He divided the space into eight columns. He labeled the columns with each of his True Titans.

"This is our War Board. It will serve as our master list. Let's begin. Seniors, come on up!"

The players jeered as the seniors advanced to the easel. Coach War looked away, turning his back to the juniors and sophomores. He pressed both of his hands against the small of his back.

"Pick a number one through ten."

The juniors and sophomores watched as Coach War pointed seven fingers down to the wood of the deck floor. The three soon-to-be seniors shouted out their guesses in rapid fire.

"Three!"

"Five!"

"Seven!"

"Seven," Coach War said with a grin, slyly revealing his hands.

The True Titan seniors each selected another senior to be on their summer lifting team. Coach War recorded the selections on the War Board. The selection process was repeated with the juniors, followed by the sophomores. The player draft went better and faster than Coach War had anticipated. When the Coach Killers were the only players remaining in the draft, the True Titans began to balk.

"I don't want any of these guys on *my* team," one senior protested.

"Me either," echoed a junior. "These guys won't do any of the work."

Coach War smiled.

"I have to deal with them," he explained. "They are members of our team too."

"But, Coach," Remmy whined. "It's not fair to the greater group."

"Actually, it *is* fair," Coach War rationalized. "Every lifting team will have some of these kids. It is your job as a True Titan to lead them. You don't want to deal with them? Get them to buy into the process. I trust all of you to do your best with these players."

And that was the end of it. Every player had a summer lifting team. Player names filled the War Board.

"That settles it," Coach War concluded. "I'll get everyone a hard copy of this. It will be your responsibility to keep track of your team's progress once summer conditioning begins. I want you to meet with your team this week. Exchange cell phone numbers, Snapchat, Instagram, Twitter, whatever, but you will be expected to communicate with your team throughout the summer. There will be awards for the team with the most lifts, highest percentage of attendance, and total weight lifted. Good luck!" He added a line from the Navy SEALs. "Because gentlemen, it pays to be a winner. Be safe at graduation parties. Remember, you have more to lose than others. Meeting adjourned."

The True Titans felt good about their team heading into summer. They left Coach War's house empowered.

Chapter Forty

Flat Tire

The Monday after graduation was finals week for the underclassmen. Test anxiety spread throughout the school, as kids worked to finish the school year. Coach War paid student complaining no attention. It was business as usual for him. While the other teachers scheduled tests for Thursday and Friday, prepping classes for their exam throughout the week, he continued to facilitate team activities in the gym.

Mrs. Riley, the Titans' Biology teacher, was as stressed as the students. She had always used finals week to cram in one final test *and* a lab. The sophomores regularly complained about her unfair rigidity. On Tuesday morning, Coach War whistled to himself as he walked down the hallway. *Too blessed to stress*, he told himself, rounding the corner, ready to start his day. His spirit dropped when he saw Mrs. Riley standing at the locker room door. Cheetah-patterned sunglasses rested on top of her head, wedged in her highlighted hair. She looked to be ready for summer too, dressed in a canary-yellow sun dress. Her black high heel shoes clacked against the tile. The tapping noise grew louder as Coach War made his way down the corridor.

I guess Mrs. War isn't the only one who taps her toe when she's angry. Coach War did his best to hide his contempt as the distance closed. He reached the door, retrieving his school keys from the front pocket of his khakis, and slid the key to his office inside the lock.

"Good morning, Mrs. Riley," Coach War said, trying to be collegial.

"It's *not* a good morning, Coach Warrington! Do you have a minute?"

He did, but he really did not want to spend it talking with Mrs. Riley. The only time she ventured outside of the science wing was when she needed supplies for an experiment.

"Well, what can I do for you?" Coach War asked, standing in the doorway.

"Two of your football players missed the Biology final," Mrs. Riley informed before listing the boys' names. They were two members of the leadership council.

Mrs. Riley continued. "Their grade is going in the gradebook as a zero. If it stays that way, they won't pass. If they don't pass, they can't play in the fall."

"A zero?" Coach War questioned, raising his level of concern. "Why? Can't they just take the final today?"

"Coach, I don't think your players *deserve* to take the final. They skipped school yesterday. A zero on my final is a natural consequence for that decision."

"How do you know they skipped school?"

"Well, I can't prove it," she backtracked. "If I could, I wouldn't be here right now."

Coach War threw up his hands.

"But some girls in their class can," she continued. "The boys said they couldn't come to school yesterday because they went to Omaha this weekend, and they had a flat tire. They didn't come to school yesterday because they were still in 'Omaha.'" Her fingers hinged, making air quotes to mock the truth.

Coach War glanced at his watch.

"But," she ranted, raising her voice, "the girls showed me pictures of them at a concert and a post on their Twitter account says they were home early yesterday morning. The tweet is time-stamped a little after 4:30 a.m." Mrs. Riley paused. She lowered her voice to finish her point. "Coach, they called themselves in, deciding to sleep all day rather than come to school."

Coach War's heart sunk. This was *not* the behavior he wanted from anyone on the team, and especially not from his True Titans. *If this is true, how can I keep these kids on the leadership council?* Coach War pushed pause. *It's Tuesday. Mitchell will be here later this morning. He'll know what to do.* He turned his attention back to Mrs. Riley.

"Thanks for letting me know about the situation. If they skipped your test, they need to be held accountable. Let me talk with Mr. Allen. Can I get back to you by the end of the day?"

Mrs. Riley relented, putting the issue to bed for the meantime.

* * *

Just after 9:30 a.m., Coach War was waiting for Mitchell in the field house atrium.

"Well this is quite a surprise!" Mitchell wheezed, reaching for Coach War's hand. With no time to waste, Coach War filled him in on the situation as they walked to the coaches' office.

"So tell me," Coach War asked his mentor bluntly. "If these boys were on your team, what would *you* do?"

"I've probably dealt with something similar before." An easy smile spread across his face. "As long as tests have existed, students have lied and cheated. Have you talked to your boys?"

"Yeah, I talked with them. They are sticking to their story. They say they were stranded in Omaha waiting for the car tire to be repaired."

"And what about checking their online account, the Instapost thingamajiggy?"

"You mean *Instagram*," Coach War corrected. "Yeah, their account is locked."

"And the teacher is not willing to work with you?"

Coach War lowered his chin, glaring at Mitchell.

"OK, OK, I had to ask. I'm trying to look at all the angles here."

The two sat in silence for a long while before Mitchell sprang off the couch.

"I've got it!" he exclaimed. "*You* give the test!"

Coach War shook his head. "No, you don't understand, that's the problem. She's not going to let them retake the final. It doesn't matter who the proctor is."

"No, *you* don't get it," Mitchell explained. "They won't be getting a *Biology* test!"

Coach War didn't follow, so Mitchell outlined his plan in detail.

"That's just crazy enough to work!" Coach War exclaimed, and now *he* was off the couch too. "Do you think Mrs. Riley will go along with it?"

"Why not? It's win-win!"

Coach War darted out of the coaches' office like a kid in a candy store, running to find Mrs. Riley. He stopped abruptly, popping his head back around the corner of the door.

"Mitchell, you're a genius."

Chapter Forty-One

"Which Tire?"

Mrs. Riley *loved* Coach War's proposal. Sitting in Mr. Allen's office after school, Mrs. Riley called the boys' parents; Mr. Allen and Coach War listened in. She explained that she had over-reacted to each parent, apologizing, then stated that she would be willing to allow them to take the Biology final after all. *But,* there would be one catch—the boys could only retake the final under Mr. Allen's supervision in the high school office. Coach War clenched his teeth during both phone calls as he waited for the parents' response. He relaxed when both parents accepted the terms of condition, each grateful their sons had the opportunity to make up the test.

At eight a.m. sharp the next morning the boys arrived at the high school office. Mr. Allen greeted them from behind the secretaries' counter.

"Glad to see you honor your commitments, guys," Mr. Allen complimented. "C'mon."

The boys smiled, nudging each other down the office hallway as they followed Mr. Allen. One texted the other from the pocket of his hoodie as they walked. "Dude, I can't believe we are going to get away with this."

Mr. Allen unlocked a door, opening a small, five-foot by five-foot room that was usually reserved for in-school suspensions. A long fluorescent light hummed to life with the flick of a switch. One boy walked in. Mr. Allen handed him a thin blue book to write in. The test was on a sheet of paper, tucked inside its light-blue cover. Mr. Allen started to walk away but caught himself and turned back.

"Cell phone, please?" Mr. Allen requested, extending his palm.

"Oh, right." The first boy complied, handing it over.

Mr. Allen walked the second young man to the end of the hallway, opening another door that belonged to a similar room.

"The doors need to stay open," he instructed the boys, standing in the hallway between the two rooms. "I'll be working in my office. Please bring me your test when you are finished."

Mrs. Riley's Biology final only consisted of one question. "The other day you said you were stranded in Omaha. You missed school because a flat tire needed to be repaired. Which tire? And on what road?"

When the boys were finished, Mr. Allen found Coach War.

"Well Coach, it looks like you'll have to find two new members for your leadership council. One wrote down that the front driver's side tire was flat. The other wrote that the back passenger's side was flat. And they had different roads. Either way, now we know the truth. I've already called the parents."

Coach War had been preparing himself for this moment. While he hated to see his players fail, and he *really* hated that Mrs. Riley was right, he appreciated how it was handled. The boys were given due process, and they were guilty.

"I guess they aren't defendable," Coach War told Mr. Allen, shaking his hand. "Thanks for working with me on this."

That afternoon, Coach War tracked down his two players individually.

"Your selfishness," Coach War explained, looking his athletes in the eye, "has jeopardized your credibility to lead. True Titans do the right thing *all* of the time. I'm disappointed in your behavior and have no choice but to remove you from the leadership council. We will promote the next two highest vote-getters to take your place."

He finished the one-sided conversation with a firm handshake.

"This hurts, but you need to learn a lesson. You are still a valuable member of our team and I expect you to lead in the locker room even if you *aren't* on our leadership council."

Each of the players had accepted the consequences of their behavior. They walked away from the conversation somberly. Coach War had not widened the plate. He could look himself in the mirror and know that the players had been given due process and that the punishment fit the crime. Justice had been served.

Chapter Forty-Two

"Winter's Coming"

For the first time in his career, Coach War actually looked forward to seeing the summer weight room numbers. He was especially interested in how his True Titans managed their teammates. Every morning, Coach War stopped by the weight room at the end of his run, where he would look at the numbers Coach Roman posted on the wall, then check in with his lifting teams.

June flew by, and soon it was time for the Warringtons' annual 4th of July vacation. He couldn't wait to spend a week with his family at Okoboji, where they could enjoy recreation and fireworks on the lake. As Laura packed for their trip, Coach War looked at the latest weight room spreadsheet from Coach Roman on his iPhone. Remmy's team was *crushing* their competition, dominating every facet of the Titans' summer lifting program. While other groups' numbers dwindled, Remmy's team continued to make gains. In fact, all ten members had *at least* 95 percent attendance, and their team average was closer to 98 percent. Coach War could not believe it. Numbers like this were unprecedented in Titan Football.

Remmy's team called themselves the "White Walkers," a reference to the highly-popular HBO series *Game of Thrones*. The show takes place mainly during the middle ages. Kings and queens use their armies to form alliances and defeat those against them as they try to control the seven kingdoms. Characters are always preparing for winters, which can last for years. One army is the White Walkers, descendants from the far north. These zombie-like fighters love winter and slay anyone in their way. Remmy was a huge fan of the show and he thought the White Walkers were bad-asses. He decided to bring the White Walkers' warrior-mentality to his lifting team, and the small unit banded together, vowing to win every team competition.

The White Walkers lifted together. They would spot each other, encourage each other, and push one another to achieve more. One team member would look at another and simply say, "Winter's Coming." This became the team's way of preparing for the upcoming season and holding each other accountable when someone was under-performing. "Winter's Coming" was a reminder that a teammate needed to change their attitude and put in the work.

You don't feel like lifting today? "Winter's Coming."

You're sore? "Winter's Coming."

It's too hot? "Winter's Coming."

You're too tired? "Winter's Coming."

Coach War was impressed with how this group policed themselves. He began recording *Game of Thrones* on his DVR just so he could talk to his players about what was happening in the show. After a couple of episodes, Coach War was hooked. He binge-watched entire seasons. He loved how Remmy used the White Walkers to connect his team and give themselves an identity.

* * *

Seeing the White Walkers numbers increase from week to week inspired Coach War. One day while on vacation as he cruised around West Lake, pulling his kids on a tube behind their family boat, a question raced through his mind. *How can I get more teams to be like the White Walkers? What can I change to increase my athletes' performance in the weight room?*

There were many boats on the water enjoying the hot July weather that day, but none more iconic than the Queen II. Commissioned in 1986, the Queen II was a replica of the late nineteenth century excursion boat that sailed the waters of Okoboji for nearly ninety years. Measuring seventy-five feet long and nineteen feet wide, the Queen II featured an open-air upper deck on top of an enclosed lower deck; it was easily the biggest boat on the water. It lumbered along, dwarfing the Warringtons' eighteen-foot speed boat. Maya, who was riding the tube, waved to the passengers as they passed. Coach War tipped his Titan Football visor to the captain of the vessel, who rang the ship's bell, acknowledging his fellow skipper.

Suddenly, Coach War was struck by an idea. *That's it,* he thought. *I can move the bell from the practice field into the weight room! Instead of ringing it when kids quit, we could ring it whenever someone sets a new personal record, increasing their max.* Coach War was confident that moving the bell would unite and motivate other groups, just as Remmy was able to motivate the White Walkers. And what better place than the weight room for players to learn how to become Titan Tough? *Perfect!* Coach War uttered, basking in his own brilliance. He envisioned the large brass bell hanging in the empty corner just outside Coach Roman's office. The familiar sound of his wife's voice interrupted his train of thought.

"Vinny!" she exclaimed.

"Huh," he responded, snapping out of his daydream.

"Are you going to go back for your daughter?"

Coach War hadn't noticed that Maya had been tossed off the tube.

"Oh, right," he said, pulling back on the arm of the boat's throttle, slowing the motor to circle around.

* * *

By Sunday afternoon, the Warrington family vacation was over. Most years, Coach War would be chomping at the bit to get back to his team and back in the weight room, already starting to stress about the upcoming season. This year, however, Laura noticed that her husband was more at ease, even peaceful. For the first time in their marriage, they went on vacation and *actually* relaxed together. The kids were exhausted after a week of fun in the sun and were sound asleep in their car seats before the Warrington family SUV had left Milford. Laura rode shotgun. She reclined in her seat, settling in for the next few hours' drive.

"Thanks for a fun week," she complimented, folding her left hand over his right hand on top of the center console.

Coach War smiled.

It was nearly dusk when the SUV pulled into the Warringtons' driveway. After hurriedly unloading, Coach War grabbed his cordless drill off the metal workbench in the garage.

"Be right back," he yelled to his wife, who was sifting through piles of dirty laundry in the laundry room just inside the garage.

"And just *where* do you think *you're* going?" she questioned.

"I have to run to school and make sure that everything is ready to go for tomorrow's lifting session."

"Vincent Warrington," his wife called after him. "We haven't been home for *ten minutes*, and you're going to leave me with the kids *and* this mess?"

"Thanks, honey, I knew you'd understand. Love you!"

He got back in the SUV and drove straight to the Titans' practice field, parking the car along the road that led back to the field house. The vehicle's headlights reflected off the large brass bell, illuminating the practice field. A purple sky darkening by the minute blanketed Coach War. Four rusty screws held the bell against the wooden fencepost. Surprisingly, three of the screws came out easily. One by one Coach War slid them into the front pocket of his shorts. The fourth screw, however, needed convincing. Increasing the torque on his drill, Coach War pushed down on the screw with all of his might.

"C'mon, c'mon," he begged, hoping it would turn before stripping out. After a little more heat and pressure, the screw twisted to the left.

"Yes!" he yelled, continuing to drill, wrapping his left hand around the bell's curve. The stubborn screw fell to the grass. Coach War dropped the drill, using both hands to catch the bell before walking it over to the front passenger side of his family's SUV. He shifted the bell to his left hand, lifting his leg to steady it against his thigh, while his right hand opened the car door. Coach War placed the bell's square mount onto the rubber floor mat, then returned home.

The next day, Coach War woke up early. The house was dark. He dressed for his daily run, then drove to the weight room. Using four new screws, he hung the bell next to Coach Roman's office under a banner that read "Remember the Titans."

The White Walkers were the first group to arrive for their workout. They stretched together in the open area that separated the squat racks from the cleaning platforms in the middle of the room. Other teams filed in as well, and soon the weight room was full.

"Whoa," Remmy marveled, noticing the bell hanging in the corner between sets. He nudged a teammate, then moved in to take a closer look. "Is that the bell from the practice field?"

"Yep," Coach War responded, admiring his latest touch. He stepped toward Remmy.

"Why's it in here?"

"Well, I've been crunching the numbers and there are a lot of guys on our team that are closing in on new PRs. I figured we need to celebrate that."

"But the bell's for quitters," Remmy reasoned.

"Not anymore."

Coach War smiled, pulling the bell's rope with three staccato jerks; he moved to the center of the room. "Gentlemen," he announced, raising his voice so that everyone could hear. "Behold, our newest piece of equipment." He pointed at the bell.

Recognizing the large brass bell, the players looked hesitant.

"The culture of our team is changing, so the purpose and location of our practice bell is changing too. From now on, this bell will not ring when someone has quit. Instead, it will chime whenever someone increases their max."

The players cheered, embracing the Titans' newest tradition.

"This bell is sacred," Coach War added, lowering his voice. "Anyone who tugs this rope is telling the world that they are becoming Titan Tough. From now on, we will recognize *success,* not weakness. Any questions?"

There were none. The players resumed their workouts. Coach War circulated from team to team.

Winter's Coming, he told himself. *It's time to sharpen the axe and get ready for battle.*

Chapter Forty-Three

"F N Gs"

Football started two weeks later with team camp. Coach War usually opened camp by introducing the coaches, team policies, and procedures to his squad in the locker room. But this year, he changed the venue to the library, one of the few rooms in the high school large enough for this team, and decided to have the True Titans lead the introductions.

Coach War stood behind the librarian's podium, projecting a Google Presentation from his laptop. The assistant coaches formed a straight line at his side, looking out at the team. The players sat in their summer lifting teams around the library's circular tables. Coach War introduced himself before bringing the eight True Titans to the front of the room.

"Gentlemen," Coach War said, looking out into the room. "This is *your* team, and here are your leaders."

Each of the True Titans introduced one of the eight assistant coaches. When the coach's name was called, he stepped out of line and raised his hand. The True Titans also introduced their lifting teams. The senior teams went first, followed by the juniors, then the sophomores. Finally, Coach War had his assistant coaches sit with the lifting teams; he brought the freshmen to the front of the room, many of whom looked like deer frozen in headlights.

"And here are the freshmen, the future of Titan Football," Coach War announced. Before he could present each newcomer, an upper-classman blurted out, "FNGs, man! Fucking new guys!"

Bursts of laughter reverberated around the library.

"None of that!" Coach War scolded, his tone short and to the point. "That kind of language will no longer be tolerated!"

"But Coach," the offender retorted, "we've *always* called the freshman FNGs. I remember when *I* was an FNG!"

Players around the room agreed with the senior.

"Well not anymore. And we are going to be more disciplined with what we say too. From now on, every four-letter word will come with the consequence of ten push-ups… payable *immediately.*" The players groaned. "And that goes for the coaching staff too."

Coach War peered deep into the eyes of the senior.

"Drop and give us ten," Coach War ordered.

The player mumbled under his breath, stretching across the floor to assume the position. He cranked out his ten push-ups, then rejoined his lifting team at their table.

"I want you to think back to when you were a freshman," Coach War explained. "You were all scared and unsure about playing high school sports. You might not have known anyone, or what to do. Maybe you were even worried about getting hurt. I want you to treat our newest members *better* than the way you would've wanted to be treated. Understood?"

"Yes, Coach," the team responded, as if answering a drill sergeant on Paris Island.

Coach War refocused his team's attention on the freshmen at the front of the room. Individuals waved after he read their name.

The second item on the preseason agenda was to review summer lifting numbers.

"As for the results of our summer lifting competition, making a clean sweep—lifting pun intended—and winning all three of our categories are the White Walkers! Please come get your prizes."

The group walked toward the podium. Coach War threw them each a baby-blue Dri-FIT shirt from a box behind the counter. "TITAN TOUGH" was written in blocky navy-blue letters across the chest. The screen print on the back of the shirt read: "Earned, Not Given."

"Two claps for the White Walkers! Ready?"

Two crisp claps pierced the atmosphere.

"Great job, guys. Winter's here!"

The White Walkers laughed, picking up on Coach War's reference to finally being in-season.

For the next thirty minutes, Coach War covered the Titan Football team handbook and answered players' questions. The presentation was old hat to the seniors; they had heard the same things now once a year for four years. Nevertheless, Coach War expected every player to follow along, reading from a hard copy. On the last page of the thick booklet was the accountability piece. No one would be allowed to practice in full pads until they had signed the receipt, acknowledging and accepting Coach War's expectations and policies. After the entire handbook had been addressed, Coach War projected the "Titan Tough" MVP on the library wall, asking the True Titans to come back up to the front of the room.

"This year, practice will look different," Coach War stated. "Every day of the week will be dedicated to one of our program's core values. Each core value has a definition, hand gesture, and short catch-phrase that will help you remember our purpose. Everything we do is about helping you become Titan Tough."

The White Walkers grunted, proudly waving their new gear.

"Each day during camp, we will learn a new core value, its gesture, and catch-phrase. We will do a small team energizer to build our synergy. By the end of camp, we will all be able to speak a new language..."

Players looked around at each other.

"Whoa, whoa, whoa," Remmy interrupted, raising his hand. "There's no way we can learn an entire language in just one week!"

The tables around the library all agreed.

"Ah, but you will," countered Coach War. "You will all be able to speak Titanic, the language of our team."

A collective "oh" filled the room.

"Players who learn Titanic will be able to recite the Titan Tough creed. If you can memorize the creed and repeat it in front of a coach, you will earn your helmet decal. If you don't want to memorize the creed, that's fine, but be ready to explain to people why your helmet is blank."

Grumbling filled the room.

"We will meet in here, in these groups, every day before camp. Is that clear?"

"Yes, Coach!"

"Good. Now let's get out to the practice field. The whistle blows in ten minutes. You are dismissed."

The players exited the library, heading down to the locker room to change into their cleats for practice. On the field, players fell into their stretching spots, forming the Titan Circle of Trust. When the alarm on Coach War's watch beeped, he yelled.

"IT'S A GREAT DAY FOR FOOTBALL!"

The players cheered.

The long tug on the whistle could only mean one thing… football season was back.

* * *

After practice, Coach War took his staff out for pizza. As they ate, they talked about all of the players who were at practice, and those who should be. After everyone had eaten, Coach War handed his assistants a laminated copy of the "Titan Tough" MVP, giving them a moment to digest the new team culture along with their food.

"This will be the key to our success this season and in the future," Coach War explained. "If we are going to hold our kids accountable for Titanic, then you will need to be as well. It might seem tricky at first, but I expect you to learn the themes, hand gestures, and catch-phrases. You should notice that every day correlates to something we already do. Tomorrow is Pack Your Own Parachute Tuesday. Practice it so you can help others. Any questions?"

There were none.

"Thanks for a great first day. Now let's get better tomorrow!" Coach War concluded. "See you in the morning."

Chapter Forty-Four

"Sharpen the Axe"

The next morning, players reported to the library, sitting in their lifting groups. Camp started at eight a.m. sharp. By 8:03, the players were looking to the assistant coaches, who were scratching their heads, unsure of where Coach War was or what he wanted the kids to do.

"Coach War has to be somewhere around here," Coach Hogan said, turning to Coach Roman. "Why else would the presentation be cued up?" He pointed to the slide titled "Titan Football Day #2" that was projected on the wall.

"Well, I don't understand this stuff well enough to present to the team. Do you?"

"No way," Coach Hogan replied, shaking his head vigorously from side to side.

The players stared at the library clock as the second hand moved past 8:05.

"Well this is a waste," one senior declared. "I'm invoking the five-minute rule." His entire table stood up to leave.

All of a sudden, Coach War shot out from behind a bookshelf in the back. He maneuvered toward the center of the room, hoisting a long wooden handle with both hands above his head. He nearly hit the projector with the red ax-head when he ran under its mount.

"Hi-yah!" Coach grunted, dropping the ax-head onto an old textbook, which he had staged earlier that morning on the table in the middle of the room. The axe made a loud thud as it collided with the thick textbook. The book flipped in the air but was otherwise undamaged.

The players screamed.

Moving the ax-head safely to the carpet, Coach War laughed maniacally.

"You should've seen your faces!" he teased, pointing to the group closest to the textbook. Coach War's entrance had caused the players at that table to scatter around the room, fleeing their table as if it were on fire. Breathing a sigh of relief, those individuals retook their seats.

Coach War composed himself. There was always method to his madness.

"Gentlemen, behold the axe." He held the axe parallel to the ground, raising it in his palms just above his shoulders. He twisted his torso back and forth so everyone in the room could see.

"But," he continued, "there's a problem with this axe. Talk at your tables. What is it?"

Small group discussions broke out at each table. Coach War weaved around the library, listening in on different hypotheses as players brainstormed the problem with the axe.

"The axe is too short," one table concluded.

"Wrong."

"The axe is too heavy," another table guessed.

"Nope, try again."

After every table guessed incorrectly, Coach War gave his team a hint.

"Look at the textbook. Now, talk in tables again. Go!"

After waiting a minute for the tables to mull over the axe and textbook, Coach War brought his team back together. "Any ideas?" he asked.

No one responded.

"OK, I'll give you another hint." Coach War lifted the textbook off the table, holding it high above his head as he paraded around the room.

The silence was broken by Remmy.

"Oooohhhh, *I* get it," he called out. Coach War pointed at him, asking him to explain his thinking.

"The axe didn't even make a mark on the textbook. It should have at least cut through the cover."

"So?" Coach War inquired.

"So," Remmy rationalized, "the axe is dull!"

"Ooohhhhs" were heard around the room as players saw the point.

"Very good," said their teacher. "Yes, this axe is dull. It looks intimidating, but it cannot serve its purpose." Over the next few minutes, Coach War told his team the story of the lumberjack. "You see," he said, reaching the end of the parable, "if we are going to accomplish our goals, then we need a sharp axe."

The players followed their leader's analogy.

"This year," Coach War unveiled, "our team motto will be... Sharpen the Axe."

Coach War walked back to the podium. He bent down behind the counter. When he popped back up, he hoisted a brand new axe toward the ceiling; the red ax-head glistened under the library lights.

"This, gentlemen, is what a *sharp* axe looks like. This will do some damage." Again he paced around the room, the axe held loosely in his palms for all to see. "This is what we are after."

Coach War placed the new axe across the middle of Remmy's table. He walked back to the podium and again reached behind the librarian's counter. This time he pulled out a large plastic bag. Coach War traveled from table to table, dropping fists full of silicone wristbands for his players to wear. On one half of the white wristband written in blue block letters was "Titan Tough"; the other half read "Sharpen the Axe." The players scrambled to secure some new team swag, fitting the silicone bands around their wrists.

Moving back over to his laptop at the podium, he clicked to the next slide, reprojecting the "Titan Tough" MVP. He pointed out that today was Pack Your Own Parachute Tuesday. Coach War defined the second core value, explaining how it would help the Titans sharpen their axe. The True Titans joined him up front, demonstrating the hand gesture and catch-phrase to the team. Coach War smiled as he watched teammates and assistant coaches partner up to practice Tuesday's theme. Finishing in the library, the team passed through the locker room on their way to the field.

Coach War had one more trick up his sleeve. Freshly taped to each player's locker was a personalized "Titan Tough" MVP sign. The players' names and numbers were printed in the corners, and the blue cardstock was laminated. A small red axe was also taped below the sign to remind everyone of the team's purpose.

Chapter Forty-Five

Pissing in The Wind

Friday night brought the end of camp, and Coach War was exhausted. His body ached, the long days in the hot sun already beginning to take their toll on him physically. He sank into the leather sectional next to his wife. Before reading, Coach War took some time to finalize the next week's practice plans, saving them on his phone. He always tried to be diligent about planning one week ahead and resisted the temptation to put this duty off until Sunday evening. Closing out of the Google Drive app, he clicked on the little blue bird pinned to the bottom of his home screen.

The Twitter timeline began with the words "In case you missed it…" The first tweet he saw was from one of the Titans' seniors. "This year we're going 13-0! All the way to the Dome! Y'all are trash. Stand back and watch us! We're on a mission! #ToAllOurHaters."

The player's tweet infuriated Coach War. The Titans had never been to the Dome, the site of the Iowa high school semi-finals and championship games, and even if they had, he still would not have approved of the arrogant message thrown out into the world by one of his team leaders. Twenty-seven other members of the team had already retweeted the post; more had liked it. Coach War clicked on the envelope in the lower right-hand corner of the app to send the player a direct message. He wanted to tell him to delete the tweet immediately, but hesitated. He closed out of the app. *E + R = O. I'm not going to let my emotions control this outcome.* He stared at the TV. *What would Mitchell do?* After a long moment, he reached a conclusion.

This is a teachable moment, Coach War decided. *Mitchell would address it in front of his team on Monday, and that's what I'll do. After practice, I'll tell the team about how to use social media and post appropriately.*

* * *

Monday marked thc start of official practice. The players donned helmets and PE clothes, running around the practice field as if they were one month into the season. They stretched together in the Titan Circle of Trust, improved during individual time on both the offensive and defensive sides of the ball, mixed in a group period where skill players were separated from linemen, and were finally brought back together for a team session. The last fifteen minutes of practice was reserved for conditioning. The players were exhausted, breathing heavily and dripping in sweat as the mid-morning sun cast down upon them. But this was the freshest their bodies would be all season. After running several sprints, Coach War gave a long tug on his whistle. His players took a knee in a semi-circle around him and the other coaches.

"Take care of your bodies," he began, looking at his defeated squad through his sunglasses. "Practice is only going to become more physical as the season goes on. You need to hydrate, eat quality foods, and get eight-to-nine hours of sleep each night, *not* next to your phone—in the grand scheme of things, your Snapchat streak is *not* important."

The players groaned.

"Put your phones away. They are your biggest distraction. Some studies indicate that the average teenager looks at their phone over one hundred times each day. That's ridiculous! If you want to be a great lumberjack, you don't have time to sharpen your axe if you reach for your phone every time it dings."

Coach War paused, looking down at his notes stored in the small notebook that he always carried to practice. After a moment, he lifted his head, shifting his attention to his team's most recent issue.

"And that brings me to social media. Social media is a powerful tool our society uses to connect with others. There is value in using it, and I'm not going to say that you *can't* have social media, but you need to be smart about what you post. Over the weekend, I read one player's post about how we are going to go undefeated."

The players looked away from Coach War, making eye contact with the senior who sent out the tweet.

"Stop putting that message out there for others to see! Do we want to go undefeated? Hell yeah, but we *don't* need to post it. What do we say on Fridays?"

The players straightened up, replying together in Titanic. "Let our pads do the talking!"

"Gentlemen," Coach War continued. "What you don't understand now is that there's something special about *this* right here." He spread his hands over the heads of his players. "Bill Gates, Warren Buffet, Jeff Bezos… they may have tons of money, but they can't *buy* a locker room celebration. They can't *buy* the special bond that lasts for years between teammates. You can't duplicate this feeling anywhere else. Everyone out there…" he preached, extending his hands to the outside of the semi-circle, "they can wait. They will be there later. If anyone on the *outside* wants to be *inside*, then they can put on the pads and show up at practice day-in and day-out too. But for right now, it's just us. Enjoy *this*… respect *this*."

The players looked around at their teammates in the semi-circle. Some nodded, others smiled. Coach War brought his message home with another analogy.

"When you piss outside, do you piss *into* the wind?"

The farm boys in the semi-circle raised their eyebrows and emphatically shook their heads.

"Why not?" asked Coach War.

"Won't the pee just blow back onto you?" Remmy asked.

"Yes! You will soak yourself and smell all day."

The players laughed.

"When you post comments about our team on social media, you are pissing in the wind. What you say blows back onto you and everyone else who is part of our Titan Football family."

He paused to heighten his message's dramatic effect.

"Remember, this team is special," Coach War reiterated, moving his arms back over the circle of players. "The world moves at such a fast pace today. Don't piss in the wind. Let our pads do the talking. We're just getting started. And if you *must* use social media, don't miss *your* life because you are too busy scrolling through someone else's."

One hundred sets of eyes were locked on Coach War.

"Good job today. Rest up, tomorrow will be tougher. As the Navy SEALs say, 'The only easy day was yesterday.' Let's get a breakdown and get out of here. Titans on three…"

The players rose to their feet. Remmy forced his way to the middle and led the charge.

"One, two, three…"

"TITANS!" the team cried, closing out their first day in the forest.

Chapter Forty-Six

Flush Mechanism

On Tuesday, Coach War welcomed Mitchell. It had been a long time since their last meeting at ChapaChino, and it was good to see him. Coach War showed Mitchell his player's post, and they talked about how the changes he had made to his team's culture had helped prepare him to effectively handle the situation. Mitchell winked at Coach War and applauded his efforts to teach young men proper twenty-first century etiquette while keeping his plate the standard size.

"That lesson will stick with those kids for the rest of their lives," Mitchell said. Reaching into his black leather bag, he handed Coach War an article he printed from ESPN, changing the subject.

"Here, I read this over the weekend and thought you'd like it. Take a minute and read it please."

Coach War leaned across the coffee table to accept Mitchell's offering and did as he was asked. The article was on Yankees rookie Aaron Judge, a hot, young hitter who had a unique way of handling the big-league pressure to produce. Before Judge stepped inside the batter's box for his next at bat, he subtly reached down and grabbed some dirt, rubbing it between his fingers. Coach War circled Judge's quote in the article where he mentioned crushing the dirt in his hands. Judge then tossed the mangled dirt aside. This routine, done before every at bat helped him release any negative thoughts from his head.

Coach War couldn't believe it. *Dirt helps?* He was amazed at how simple this idea was.

Judge explained that if nothing else, rubbing dirt through his hands gave him a second or two to slow the game down. But dirt was just the start of Aaron Judge's routine. The article went on to explain that before every game he chewed two pieces of Dubble Bubble and would keep gnawing on it until he made his first out. And, when an inning was over, he would purposefully mosey slowly toward the dugout from right field, the closest position to the Yankees bench, until the center and left fielders ran in so that he could give them some encouragement.

When he was done reading, Coach War dropped the article to his side and looked at Mitchell.

"So? What do you think?"

"I think it's interesting," Coach War replied.

"Can you use it with your team?"

Coach War was unsure. "I don't know how."

"Why don't you have your players establish their own pre-play routine? There are three parts to every great routine… the trigger, the event, and the response."

Coach War liked the idea of every Titan crafting their own pre-play routine.

"You could also have them come up with a personal flush mechanism," Mitchell suggested. "A mental reset button for when things go wrong."

Coach War rubbed his chin.

"After all, every play in football has its own routine. The trigger is the huddle. The team stands in a circle, looking at the quarterback, who is usually in the middle. The QB is the only one who talks; he delivers the play call. After it is said and repeated, the signal caller sends everyone to the line with a cue like 'Ready. Break!' Then, at the line of scrimmage, the quarterback has another verbal cue for his teammates… the cadence. Calling out, 'Ready. Set. Hit!' the offense knows when to go because of all the reps they have practiced before the game."

Coach War nodded along; Mitchell's analysis was spot-on.

"The part your athletes are missing, however, is the flush mechanism. As a leader, you can create a routine to help your kids stay the course. Whatever the result of the previous play was, if you develop a flush mechanism, your team will be able to keep forging ahead. It doesn't have to be complicated. After all, Aaron Judge's flush mechanism is dirt."

Mitchell returned to the article, lifting his reading glasses from around the collar of his shirt; he pressed them against his nose to read Judge's quote written in bold near the end of the article.

"This struck me," Mitchell began, clearing his throat. "'The mental game is what separates the good players from the great players. So anything I can do to get that mental edge to help me stay my best, I'm gonna try and do it.'"

Coach War used his pen to engulf the quote inside a large circle.

"What I think Aaron Judge is saying," Mitchell concluded, "is that if you want your team to be elite, as a coach, *you* need to give them a mental edge. Give them a flush mechanism, something they can use to get mentally ready for the next rep."

"But how?" Coach War pleaded. "I understand that a flush mechanism is part of peak performance, but it's easier for Aaron Judge who has all of the resources of the Yankees. How the heck do you create a flush mechanism for a high school kid? Any ideas?"

Mitchell coughed into his sleeve. He took a small sip of water from his plastic water bottle, then eased back into the webbing of the couch. Removing his glasses, he closed his eyes. He tilted his head toward the ceiling before answering Coach War's question.

"Oh, I'm sure you'll think of something. You always do." Mitchell took a deep breath, reopening his eyes. He glanced at his watch and saw that their time together was about to expire for the week. "Well," Mitchell said, slapping his palms onto his knees before staggering off the couch, "my wife will be expecting me at ChapaChino." He leaned forward to shake Coach War's hand. "See you next week, partner. I'm proud of you. And don't *flush* that!"

Chapter Forty-Seven

Shred It!

Later that week, the preseason state rankings were released. Sportswriters for the major newspapers around the state looked at last season's results, team rosters and schedules and published their predictions for the upcoming season. The day the preseason rankings came out, Coach Roman stopped by the locker room. He carried a rolled-up newspaper that swayed back and forth in his left hand with each step he took; Coach War was standing in the hallway and could see him coming from a mile away.

"Have you seen this?" Coach Roman asked, unrolling the wad of paper and shoving the local high school sports section in Coach War's face. "Looks like Lone Tree is predicted to win the district… again."

Coach War snatched the paper out of Coach Roman's hand, squeezing it in his grip. He scanned through the predictions. When he read how the writers felt about the Titans' future, his head dropped. According to the sports writers, the Titans would finish at the bottom of their district.

"Can I have this?" Coach War asked.

"I brought it for you. I knew you'd want to see it."

"Thanks. I've got plans for this article," he said in a sly voice, rerolling the paper before tucking it into the back pocket of his khakis.

* * *

Wednesday marked the first day of school for the new year. Once again, kids fluttered about in the hallway, many wearing a fresh fall look. Energy flowed throughout the building. The day flew by, and Coach War was glad to be back; it was nice to have something other than football to focus on. After his last class that afternoon, Coach War beat the players to the locker room.

"We will begin practice today in the library," he announced, hanging a sign on the locker room door. Players reported to the locker room ready for practice, only to have to turn around and head down the hall to the school's media center. They sat at their familiar tables in their regular groups. When the room was nearly at capacity, Coach War spoke.

"Gentlemen, today is 'Why Not? Wednesday.' One of the things that our team has been missing in recent years is mental toughness, and being Titan Tough is about being mentally tough as well as physically tough."

Coach War paused, taking a pull from his water bottle. Even though the air conditioning was on, with over one hundred bodies in the room, the August air was stifling.

"One way to practice mental toughness is to have a short-term memory. Players who perform at high levels have the ability to hit reset, to flush the outcome of one play and be ready to move on to the next. Here is Aaron Judge." Coach War clicked a button on his laptop. The Yankee ball-player projected against the library wall. Coach War proceeded to describe his at-bat routine, explaining how dirt was his flush mechanism.

"Now, I want you to talk in your table groups about the following question… if you have a bad play, what do you say to yourself so you are able to move on and focus on the next one? True Titans, you share first. Ready? Go!"

The room filled with voices. Coach War paced from table to table, listening in. After everyone at a table had shared, the table leader gave Coach War a thumb's up. When the majority of the tables were done, Coach War circulated back to the podium. The players continued to talk amongst themselves. Using a learning strategy from his instructional coach, he brought his team back together as a large group.

"Flat tire," he announced, "in three… two… one… shhhhhhhhhhhhhh."

Coach War pushed oxygen out of his lungs forcefully; it sounded as if air was escaping from a punctured tire. By the time his lungs were empty, Coach War expected that individual conversations would cease.

"Let's discuss. What do you tell yourself after a bad play to get ready to play the next down?"

"I shake my head," one player shared aloud.

"And that helps you refocus?" Coach War asked.

"I don't know," he shrugged.

Another player raised his hand.

"I tell myself to forget about it."

"Good," Coach War affirmed. He called on another athlete.

"I say 'flush it,'" another one offered.

Laughter echoed around the room. His teammates knew that "flush it" *really* meant another "f"-word, but by saying it this way, he could avoid push-ups.

Coach War quieted the room.

"If our axe is going to stay sharp this year, then we have to be able to move on when bad things happen. And I promise you, gentlemen, bad things *will* happen over the course of the season. Our teams haven't been able to overcome adversity in the past."

Unrolling the paper Coach Roman had given him earlier in the week, Coach War held up the district predictions for all to see. He felt like Mufasa in *The Lion King* presenting Simba to the pride for the first time.

"Here are the preseason predictions for every team across the state. Some of you may have seen this. I was handed this by a staff member earlier this week."

Coach War pointed to his team's prediction. Grabbing a black Sharpie off the librarian's counter, he marked the newspaper, filling the page with a "4" and a "5." When he was done, he held it up again.

"Four and five. That's all the local sportswriters believe in you. They don't even think you are a winning team."

Coach War paused for a moment for dramatic effect. He reached behind the counter, lifting up a large black object.

"Well here's how much *I* believe in *them!*" He crumpled the paper, stuffing it into the top of the object. A loud motor kicked on, and the players realized that it was a shredder. It hummed, sucking the paper in, carving it into ten thousand unrecognizable pieces.

"If you want to become Titan Tough, you need to be able to shred anything that could impact the success of this team."

Coach War paused, letting his team absorb this concept.

"See something negative on social media? Shred it!"

"Make a mistake on the field? Shred it!"

"Someone has something to say in the hallway? Shred it!"

"Fail a math test? Shred it!"

"Your girlfriend wants to break up with you? Shred it!"

"It's all noise! I don't care about *noise*. I care about *you*. Don't let the things you can't control determine the success of this team!"

Coach War paused again, taking a sip from his water bottle.

"What you *choose* to listen to fuels your subconscious. You can buy into the hype, *or* you can shred it. If you can ignore the noise, or the haters, as you might say..." he smiled when others began to laugh, "... you will keep your axe sharp and stay focused on the task that is in front of you. When you ignore the noise, you can keep chopping down trees."

Heads nodded around the room, letting Coach War know they understood his message.

"There are a lot of people who are counting us out of the race. Don't listen to them. Take their comments and shred them. Focus on us. Focus on the process of being Titan Tough. Everything else will sort itself out. From now on, this shredder will be in our locker room. It will be the first thing you see when you walk in the door. Anytime someone says something negative to you about our team, I want you to write what they say on a piece of paper and shred it immediately! Keep our house clean, nothing toxic… good vibes only!"

"Let's start as a team. I want everyone to write down a negative comment right now. It can be something you have said to yourself or something you heard from others."

The assistant coaches passed out pieces of scratch paper and pencils, making sure every table had some.

Tension around the room evaporated as players wrote down negative thoughts on the paper slips. When they finished writing, Coach War invited his kids to come up to the counter and shred their comments. When everyone was done, Coach War reiterated that it was Why Not? Wednesday.

"CAN WE WIN THE DISTRICT?" he yelled at his team.

"WHY NOT!" the team screamed back.

The Titans stormed out of the library and had one of their best practices of the season.

Chapter Forty-Eight

The Oyster and the Pearl

Coach War found it hard to sleep the night before the first game of the season. In an attempt to conserve his energy, knowing that his body needed rest, he did his best to quiet his mind, hoping to capture a few hours of sleep. Laura nudged him throughout the night as he tossed and turned. Eventually he traded his pillow for his legal pad. Standing under the glow of the cabinet lights in the kitchen, Coach War organized his thoughts, penciling out some ideas for tomorrow night's pregame speech.

Titan game day was unlike any other. Coach War's energy surged at the morning pep rally. Every Titan started the day by reporting to the gym. The band entertained students and staff filing in, playing songs like Carly Rae Jepsen's "Call Me Maybe" and "Thrift Shop" by Macklemore. When the bleachers were full, Mr. Allen walked out to midcourt, holding a microphone. The band broke into the school song, causing the student body to rise and clap along with the drumline.

"Gooooooooood morning, Titans!" Mr. Allen said into the microphone, his voice echoing over the gym speakers. The students applauded as the bass drummer belted out three quick raps. Mr. Allen's pep rally script was always the same. First, the cross-country coach would say a few words, followed by the volleyball coach, with the cheerleaders performing between each speech. Coach War was always last on the agenda.

"And now," Mr. Allen announced, "please help me welcome our football coach to the floor!"

The band broke into "All I Do Is Win." Coach War mouthed the lyrics to the chorus to himself as he walked.

"All I do is win, win, win, no matter what, got money on my mind, I can never get enough. And every time I step up in the building everybody's hands go up…"

The band abruptly stopped. Coach War peered out at the student body, which was crammed into the middle section of the bleachers. Every students' hands were up, extending toward the ceiling. Standing at midcourt, Coach War shook Mr. Allen's right hand, taking the microphone from his left.

"IT'S A GREAT DAY FOR FOOTBALL!"

The students roared, remaining standing but putting their arms down. Three more raps from the bass drum belted across the gym.

A genuine smile crept across Coach War's face; he loved Titan game day. He soaked in the ambiance, admiring the game jerseys his players wore to school on Fridays in the fall. Modeled after Penn State's classic look, the Titans' home game jersey was solid navy blue, featuring twelve-inch, powder-blue numbers sewn onto the chest and back. Smaller four-inch numbers were placed on each shoulder, just above the tri-cep. A powder-blue Nike swoosh above the heart completed the look. Coach War loved how the block of uniforms, sitting front and center, popped off the bleachers. "Winners sit up front," he believed, advice he shared with his team, and there they were. After a moment, he spoke into the microphone.

"Tonight, we are going to play with a sharp axe. All year we've waited for another opportunity to play, and now it's finally here."

Three more raps on the bass drum were punctuated by a rhythmic high kick from the cheerleaders along the court's baseline.

"When you come to watch us play, I want you to leave saying that is the grittiest team I've ever seen. We're not just going to play tough,"

Coach War said with a grin, pausing for dramatic effect, "tonight we're going to play *Titan Tough!*"

The drumline roll-off led into the school song. Coach War fed off the pep rally's energy throughout the day at school.

* * *

That night in the coaches' office, Coach War paced, glancing at a small, black clock above the door that counted down the time remaining until kickoff in bright red numbers. The locker room was silent. Each athlete had their own pre-game routine. Some players sat at their lockers with their earbuds in; others had the team trainer tape their ankles. Gatorade bottles circulated around the locker room, being passed from player to player. Coach War stepped through the door from the coaches' office to the locker room. He made his way to the open space in the center. The players squeezed together along the wooden bench that ran in front of the row of lockers. They fixed their eyes on their leader.

"Gentlemen, tonight there will be two kinds of people on the field… oysters and pearls."

He paused.

"Do you know how a pearl is made? Every pearl starts out as a speck, possibly a tiny grain of sand or particle of food that becomes trapped inside an oyster. The oyster covers the particle with nacre, the same mineral substance it uses to build its shell. The oyster grinds, adding layers and layers of nacre, until one day, it crystalizes into a pearl. This process is not quick or easy. One pearl takes an oyster at least six months to make and could take as long as two years."

Coach War paused again, staring into his player's eyes.

"You see, if given a choice between an oyster and a pearl, most people are only interested in the pearl. After all, pearls are valuable. Its luster shines, making it beautiful and highly prized. Others judge a pearl. The more round it is, the more valuable it becomes."

The Titans were mesmerized.

"But the pearl doesn't actually *do* anything. It's just lucky. It was a small fleck, floating across a massive ocean and would've dissolved had it not come into contact with the oyster. Inside the oyster, the pearl lives a comfortable existence. It's nestled away from the dangers of the outside world, protected by the oyster's hard exterior. The pearl is pretentious and fragile. If it were to become damaged, it would lose its value. But until then, it's highly sought after."

Coach War stopped, taking a deep breath before segueing to the oyster.

"On the other hand, the oyster is easily passed over. It is unattractive and meaningless in value. It's just an oyster, right?"

Some of the players laughed.

"WRONG! The oyster is a fighter! It's a survivor. It faces challenges head on. Millions of years of evolution have given the oyster the ability to protect itself. And, because of that adaptation, it has something to offer the world. It contributes. An oyster can take a small, meaningless speck of matter and transform it into a masterpiece. And it can do it over and over again. While *everyone* looks out for the pearl, the oyster has to fend for itself."

The Titans were silent.

"So, what's the difference between an oyster and a pearl?"

Pause.

"Grit," he replied, answering his own question. "Mother Nature *forces* the oyster to have grit."

Coach War's voice reached a crescendo.

"Tonight, be like the oyster! Don't just stand there looking good in your uniform... contribute! Fearlessly stand in the middle of the ocean and embrace the challenges that come your way. When adversity hits, shred it! Use each other as layers of protection, and be gritty. Relentlessly grind out pearl after pearl! Go grit 'em!"

The players rose to their feet, screaming as they exited the locker room in a frenzy. They each pounded the "Titan Tough" logo Coach War had painted above the doors that led to the game field.

Three hours later, when the doors burst open again, the Titans were louder than when they had left. "Congratulations" by Post Malone played over the locker room speakers. The players danced, individually at first, then in a large circle. They belted out the chorus together at the top of their lungs: "Now they always say congratulations. Worked so hard, forgot how to vacation. They ain't never had the dedication. People hatin' say we changed and look we made it. Yeah we made it."

The team celebrated together throughout the night. Coach War's squad was 1-0.

Chapter Forty-Nine

Spread Hope

Coach War was scowling at his desk on Tuesday morning. His eyebrows furrowed, and his mouth was pinched and closed, but his eyes were concentrating on a page of the book he was reading. He had lost track of time and did not see Mitchell enter the locker room.

"Whatcha reading?" Mitchell said in his familiar upbeat voice.

"Oh," Coach War responded, "this book that was assigned to us last week in professional development. *Welcome back to school*, I guess," he mocked, sliding a small paper bookmark inside the spine. The book thudded against his desk as he set it down.

"Ah, *Mindset* by Dweck," Mitchell said with admiration, reading the cover.

"Yeah, it sucks. I have a lot on my plate right now, and now I have to read *this*," Coach War complained, leaning back in his chair at his desk.

Mitchell smiled, standing in the doorway as he pointed at Coach War.

"Sounds like *you* are operating in a fixed mindset currently."

"Wait, you know about this book?"

"Of course. I think Carol Dweck's research is powerful. As a leader, you need to have a growth mindset. Every challenge, obstacle, setback, roadblock you encounter offers a lesson. Failure is an opportunity, *not* a burden."

Coach War felt guilty; he hung his head, knowing that Mitchell was right.

"Remember," Mitchell reminded him, "it's about the journey, not the result. Instead of groaning about PD, try changing your mindset. Embrace the opportunity to grow as a leader."

Coach War stood. Mitchell stepped back into the locker room, and the pair walked past the players' lockers toward the coaches' office, the traditional setting for their weekly meetings.

"Having a growth mindset is powerful," Mitchell continued.

"OK, OK," Coach War said, sitting down on the couch across from Mitchell. "I will have a better attitude about my professional responsibilities."

"Good, but there is a bigger point here. Have you ever considered *why* teachers participate in PD?"

"Because the state makes us?" Coach War said.

"Well, yes," Mitchell agreed. "But the purpose of professional development is to improve instruction which, in turn, will lead to greater student achievement."

"I get it," Coach War whined. "I already told you I would approach my work with a better mindset. Sheesh." He exhaled. "Why does it matter to you anyway?"

"Because just having a growth mindset is not enough. There is a second part to it."

Coach War looked across at his mentor. He tilted his head away from Mitchell. *Of course there's more… there's always more.*

"The second part of having a growth mindset is hope that the future will be better than the current reality. You see, every leader's job should be to spread hope."

Mitchell paused before continuing to make his point.

"Do you remember the Cold War?"

"Ummm, yes, but I was a little kid. How could the Cold War possibly relate to growth mindset?"

"One of the most hopeful leaders in our nation's history was President John F. Kennedy. Without his brief leadership, the Cold War may have gone drastically different. When I was in high school, people lived in fear of the possibility of a nuclear war. What I remember most about that time was the space race. Like President Kennedy, I was fascinated by the thought of putting a man on the moon. When I was a senior, in 1962, the United States was losing the space race. The Soviets had already successfully launched a satellite *and* had a man orbit the earth. Most Americans lived in fear that the Soviet Union was spying on us. There wasn't much hope."

Coach War leaned forward in his seat, his eyes locked on Mitchell. He had not thought about the Cold War since he had studied it in high school.

"In 1962, President Kennedy inspired the nation with the bold announcement that before the decade was over, the United States would go to moon. The American people responded. Although President Kennedy did not live to see it, on July 20, 1969, his vision of hope was realized. You see, Coach, a growth mindset alone doesn't mean *anything*. But, if you can inspire others by spreading hope, you can accomplish the unthinkable."

Chapter Fifty

Climb the Highest Mountain

The Titans won their second game. Coach War shared his team's success with Mitchell the next Tuesday. Mitchell was happy for him but reminded Coach War that his team had started 4-0 last season, only to stumble after losing sight of their goal.

"Coach, I used to tell my team that the season was like climbing Mount Everest."

"How is football season like climbing Mount Everest?" Coach War asked, sitting across from Mitchell in the coaches' office.

"See, there's another lesson to be learned from President Kennedy's moon speech. Do you have your computer handy?"

"Be right back," Coach War said, leaving the coaches' office to retrieve his laptop from his desk. When he returned, he sat next to Mitchell on the couch.

"Punch up the speech. Have you seen it?"

Coach War shook his head, typing into the YouTube search bar. He clicked on the first link to appear, a two-minute segment of the president's speech.

"Now, as we watch, I want you to tell me what you hear."

Coach War played the clip. President Kennedy's speech was annotated with text, making it easier to understand his message. His thick Boston accent rang out through the laptop's speakers.

"We meet in an hour of change and challenge..." President Kennedy chimed.

Coach War sat up on the couch, intently watching the video. Mitchell stared at the ceiling thinking he must have heard this speech a thousand times. Mitchell's mind floated back to the time the speech was delivered. When the clip had concluded, Coach War closed his laptop, setting it on the coffee table that separated the two couches.

"So," Mitchell asked, "aside from spreading hope across the United States, what message did you hear?"

"Going to the moon would be a choice. The United States would do it not because it was easy, but because it was hard."

"Right! So why should we climb Mount Everest?" Mitchell questioned, checking for understanding the way he had years ago in his Language Arts classroom.

"Not because it is easy, but because it is hard," Coach War repeated.

"Good. President Kennedy is talking about what business leader Rory Vaden calls the 'Pain Paradox.' To paraphrase, Vaden suggests that the short-term *easy* leads to the long-term *hard*, while the *short-term* hard leads to the *long-term* easy."

Coach War did not understand.

"Think of your team just two seasons ago." Mitchell paused.

Coach War cringed.

"I wasn't around then, but I'm betting your plate was *pretty* wide, and you let your team settle for the short-term easy."

Coach War nodded.

"Since then, however," Mitchell added, "you have done the short-term difficult, investing in your program's culture to change the experience your kids have. I'm proud of you for that, and Vaden's Pain Paradox says that the future will be easier because you've done that legwork."

Coach War smiled.

"So, I'll ask you again, why climb the highest mountain?"

"Not because it is easy, but because it is hard, I get that," Coach War responded.

"Well, it takes time to climb Mount Everest," Mitchell continued. "There's a process. Coach, we live in a society that wants results *yesterday* with minimum personal investment along the way."

Coach War understood this statement perhaps better than Mitchell. Again, he reflected on what it was like to coach the twenty-first century athlete.

"But," Mitchell explained, "you can't just show up at the base of the mountain and do it all in one day. Every year, people try to reach the summit but can't because they don't have the right approach to accomplish the task. Do you know how much time it actually takes?"

Coach War shook his head.

"Experts recommend taking sixty to seventy days. Climbers set up base camps at four different stages throughout their journey, one at the mountain's base, then three camps as they climb. The climbers stay at each camp for several days, allowing for their bodies to adjust to the conditions and altitude. When they reach the final base camp, the summit is in sight. Still, climbers need to plan at least three summit attempts. Nothing is guaranteed. Those who rush this process will never realize their dreams."

Coach War was fascinated. He knew that climbing Mount Everest was a serious endeavor, but he didn't know it took *that* long.

"Coach, your season is Mount Everest. Everyone wants to get to the top, but there's a process that must be followed to successfully reach the summit. You need to set up base camps along the way and give yourself time to acclimate to your surroundings. Sixty days is about the duration of the season isn't it?"

Coach War nodded. There were nine regular season games each year, played weekly for about two months.

"You know where you want to go, right?" Mitchell asked.

"Yeah, to the playoffs," Coach War responded.

"And you know your final destination?"

"Yeah, the Dome. "

"Then focus on what you need to do to reach the next base camp on your journey. Don't worry about your season record. Focus on going 1-0 each week, and then take time to acclimate. If you stumble along the way, regroup at the final base camp and plan multiple summit attempts."

Be 1-0 each week, Coach War thought. He liked Mitchell's approach. This would be an easy sell to his team. Every Mirror Test Monday they would self-reflect, a form of acclimating to their mountain. If they were 1-0 that week, they could climb to the next camp; if not, they would take more time and try again soon. *Climbing Mount Everest is like the lumberjack working in the forest; acclimating at base camp is similar to the lumberjack sharpening his axe.*

"We find ourselves at a base camp currently," Coach War noted.

"You're off the ground, that's a start. The hard part will be to *not* look ahead. Remember, the wins are fleeting. Enjoy the journey."

"I promise," Coach War agreed. "Just like the lumberjack working in the forest, I'll only focus on one tree at a time."

Chapter Fifty-One

Stay Away from the Rat Poison

The Titans had steadily climbed Mount Everest, going 1-0 in each of their first four games; they used the Mirror Test to build a new base camp every Monday. The average margin of victory for the team during this stretch was greater than two touchdowns. Coach War envisioned his team halfway up the mountain. The climb had been easy to this point, and it had been easy to acclimate. The next stretch, however, would be one of the toughest of the season.

Week five was rivalry week versus Lone Tree. Just like last year, both teams were undefeated, and the winner would be in sole control of first place in the district standings. The second half of last year's game still haunted Coach War, so he spent the majority of the week in isolation. After all, it was that game that had proved his team needed more leadership and mental training. Had the Titans won last season, he might not have made any changes to his team's culture.

"I feel good heading into this test," Coach War told his wife while making dinner together on Sunday night. "But, man, Lone Tree looks fast on film."

"You think you can finally get 'em?" Laura asked.

"I think so, but we can't afford any mental mistakes. That second half *killed* our chances last year. I don't want to experience *that* ever again."

"Well then," she reasoned, "maybe I shouldn't show you this." She held out her phone for her husband to see. On the screen was an article from that day's newspaper. In bold letters, the headline read: "Titans' Turn to Take Lone Tree."

"Where did you get that?" he asked, stopping dead in his tracks.

"My sister saw it and forwarded me the link. She's really happy for you. You've been getting some great press lately. Many of the writers are starting to rank your team as one of the best in the state. Exciting, don't you think?"

Coach War didn't know what to say. If his wife had seen the article, then his players probably had too. He stood there dumbfounded, snarling his upper lip. He chewed on what to do while seasoning the meat, placing the pan in the oven. This was not the message he wanted his team to hear.

On Mirror Test Monday during rivalry week, Coach War decided that he wasn't going to ignore the noise. He addressed his team in Coach Hogan's room after school. When he turned out the lights and started the projector, the team broke into their Monday ritual.

"Friday night's over, it's in our past," they called in unison. "Let's look to game day and sharpen our axe!" Then it was Coach War's turn.

"We finished last week 1-0, but the eye in the sky doesn't lie. Let's take a look." Coach War started the new Hudl playlist, which contained some of the Titans' most explosive plays so far this season. One of the first cut-ups was a seventy-three-yard touchdown pass. Coach War paused the film before showing the play. "Here's our biggest play of the season to date."

The players watched as Ron Stenson, number eighty-seven, a Titan wide receiver, hauled in a long pass down the sideline that went for a touchdown. After Stenson crossed the goal line, Coach War rewound the clip, pausing the film to break it down.

"There. Do you see it?"

The players were motionless.

"You don't see it? The DB stumbles. It's not much, but it allows Ron to get a free release down the sideline. The ball is on the money, the safety doesn't get there in time, and we are off to the races for six points."

Stenson beamed when Coach War started the clip over again.

"If the defender doesn't lose his footwork, then Ronny never makes that play."

The team agreed, nodding their heads.

"Now, Stenson, it's a heck of a play, and you still had to catch the ball and run to the end zone, but it's really the DB who made that score possible. What's the lesson?"

Coach War took a long pull from his water bottle; the players were silent.

"Was that play fun? Sure. Athletic? You bet. But you need to know that you're never as *good* as you think you are."

Coach War paused, exiting out of the most recent playlist. He clicked on another playlist, showing his team all of the penalties and turnovers they had committed in the first four games.

"But, you're also never as *bad* as you think you are. These are some of the stumbles we have had along our climb." The players watched as their teammates jumped offsides, ran wrong routes, and fumbled the ball.

"You see," Coach War continued, letting the tape roll, "we aren't perfect. We've had to rely on our grit to overcome adversity in each of our first few games. We didn't let one single play beat us. Am I happy about these errors? Hell no! But, there's no such thing as a perfect game in football. It just comes down to this… when adversity hits, will you crumble or will you choose to be resilient?"

Coach War paused, taking another pull from his water bottle. He lifted a newspaper page off Coach Hogan's desk, unfolding it, holding it up for all in the room to see.

"Has anyone seen this?"

The players nodded their heads, smiling, nudging their neighbors, confident that the sports writers had finally recognized their team efforts.

"This…" Coach War stated in a slow, clear voice, "…this is rat poison!"

The players looked around the room, narrowing their eyes in confusion.

"You need to listen to *us*," Coach War said, pointing to the coaching staff along the side wall. "*Not* this!"

Low-level grumbling spread throughout the room. Remmy spoke up.

"But, Coach, what's so bad about a little good publicity? Isn't it nice to be recognized?"

"It is a nice article," Coach War explained, "but it won't help you on Friday night. When you only listen to how good you are, and all that stuff people tell you when you're winning, it's like eating rat poison."

The newspaper fell innocently on top of Coach Hogan's keyboard at his desk. Coach War's speech slowed, and the harshness of his tone faded. He casually moved from behind Coach Hogan's desk to sit on top of an unoccupied desk in front of his team.

"Last year, heading into the Lone Tree game, I ate the rat poison. I believed we were better than we were. We hung with them until half, but when our weaknesses were exposed by a sound football team, I didn't know how to handle it."

Tears welled in Coach War's eyes.

"The thing is, gentlemen, I had to learn the hard way that you're never as *good* as you think you are, and you're never as *bad* as you think you are. I wish I could go back in time and do it differently."

Coach War spoke openly and honestly, allowing himself to be vulnerable, from the heart.

"Guys, I'll personally guarantee that you don't want to live with the pain of regret. Serving my suspension was one of the hardest things I've ever had to do. Over the past year, I've thought a lot about that game and about my behavior. Here's what I have concluded. Most people will handle failure the same way. It will motivate them, and they'll push themselves harder than they ever have before. American history has countless examples of this. But you know what I think is *more* important?"

The players were stunned. They had never heard Coach War talk like this before. Ever.

"I think it's more important to know how to handle *success.* I didn't handle success very well last year. I ate the rat poison, and it cost me. If we are going to be successful on game day, we all need to focus on our process and do what it takes to go 1-0."

Coach War rose off the desk, lifting the newspaper off Coach Hogan's desk.

"You can't do that if you read this."

A shrill noise cut through the room as players watched him tear the page in half.

"Shred it. Stay away from the rat poison."

Chapter Fifty-Two

Rivalry Redemption

The rivalry game against Lone Tree was a hard-fought battle going back and forth; it was a game for the ages. As the final quarter dwindled down, the score remained tied. When the clock hit zeroes, play was suspended for a brief timeout. An excited, high-pitched voice echoed across the stadium's public-address system.

"All right, Titan fans, free football!"

The crowd cheered.

Both teams made their way to their respective sidelines. The players only had enough time to have a short chat with their coaches and to take a quick drink from the team's Gatorade bottles. For the captains, however, there was no time to relax. They walked from the sideline to midfield to meet the officials for the overtime coin toss. When both teams' captains were within arms-length of each other at the fifty-yard line, the head official reached into his pocket and pulled out a small coin.

"OK, guys," he commended, "great game so far. Let's have a clean finish. Titans, you are the home team, so you will call it in the air."

The silver coin sparkled as it flipped above their heads into the Friday night lights.

"Tails never fails!" Remmy called out.

As the coin descended toward the ground, all of the eyes at midfield dropped with it, each pair zooming in on the blades of grass that surrounded the silver coin.

"Tails it is," declared the white hat. "Titans, what do you want to do?"

"Defense," Remmy selected.

"Lone Tree, which end zone would you like to defend?"

"We'll defend the south end zone."

"OK, fellas, shake hands and get ready for a memorable finish."

As the opposing captains exchanged grips, the head official signaled the results of the coin toss to the crowd. The Titans' school song roared from the pep band in the stands; captains rejoined their teams on the sidelines. Coach War gathered around his defense at the twenty-five-yard line.

"Here we go, Oysters, let's finish! Go grit 'em!" He clapped, cheering his players on. The defense jogged onto the field. Coach War crouched down; his hands rested on his knees, and he was clenching his teeth. He looked like a golfer lining up a late-round birdie putt. Coach War lived for this moment. He felt more alive than ever. There was no other place this feeling could be duplicated.

The Titans' defense had their backs against the wall. When Lone Tree broke their offensive huddle, the Titans crowded the line of scrimmage. A middle linebacker recognized Lone Tree's formation from film study. He barked out an order, stunting the defensive alignment during the quarterback's cadence. All week the Titans had scouted this formation and were anticipating the sweep to the left that was about to occur.

Lone Tree was unprepared for the Titans' shift and could not account for the extra man who came unblocked off the edge. The running back had nowhere to go. He froze, standing in the backfield like a deer caught in the headlights. The Titans' nose tackle crossed the face of the defender responsible for him, tracking the ball carrier's back hip. He lowered his level, aligning his facemask to the football's laces. He felt like a sniper, zeroing in on a target, framing him within his scope's crosshairs. The impact of the collision sent the running back to the ground. The ball popped out, turning end over end in the air.

Coach War saw it happen in slow motion from the sideline. First, the ball hit the turf, then a scrum of players hurled toward it, creating a dog pile around the fifteen-yard line. The referees jumped in, pulling people off of each other, sifting to the bottom of the pile. The last player on the turf was a Titan. Coach War saw him curled up in the fetal position, lying face down, motionless, with his back to the Titans' sideline. Coach War exhaled and rose off his knees.

The head official reached down and took the ball from the Titan. The Titan sprung up, and the white hat returned to an upright position, raising an object for all to see. It was the football. The Titans had recovered the loose ball. Coach War slammed his fists into the air, yelling into the microphone of his headset. Coach Hogan in the booth didn't mind because he was yelling too. The referee waved his arms, signaling the end of Lone Tree's possession. It was now first down, Titans. The crowd erupted.

"Offense, offense," Coach Roman barked down the bench, notifying everyone of the change of possession. The starting offense surrounded Coach War on the sideline. Coach Roman counted eleven players, then shooed them onto the field. "Your turn! Let's go!"

Coach War wrapped his arm around the horse collar of his quarterback's jersey, giving him the play call.

"Pro left, fade right," Coach War commanded. He patted the quarterback's butt as the young man trotted away from the sideline toward the huddle. When the ball was snapped, the back-shoulder pass to the corner of the end zone fell incomplete but drew a penalty flag, giving the Titans first and goal on Lone Tree's five-yard line.

This is it. Don't get fancy now, Coach War told himself. *Trust your players.*

Coach War reached for the nearest wide receiver in the Titans' rotation, pulling him in tight to whisper into his ear.

"Give it to Remmy?" he asked his assistant coaches, speaking into the headset. Everyone agreed. He looked into the wide receiver's eyes, giving him the play. "Pro right, thirty-two iso on set."

The wide receiver jogged onto the field, meeting his quarterback just inside the hash, away from the huddle. Coach War watched him whisper into his quarterback's earhole. Walking back to the huddle, the quarterback gave the call to the team. A thunderous clap dispersed the tight group, and the offense slowly made their way together to the line of scrimmage. The quarterback glanced each way down the line, making sure everyone was set before beginning his cadence.

"Ready. Set!"

The center snapped the ball, leading a push to the goal line. The fullback followed his center's butt, leading up on the middle linebacker. Remmy lunged forward, lifting the ball into open air. Coach War covered his mouth, turning away as the ball slipped from his hand, falling to the turf. Players from both teams dove into a dog pile in hopes of recovering the loose ball.

No call was made. Pushing the players back to their respective huddles, the white hat gathered his crew at the goal line to confer on the proper call. Lone Tree's offense was running onto the field, anticipating another offensive series. Coach War looked at the melee, while Coach Roman held Titan players back. After a long conference, the head official stepped out of the tight circle and blew his whistle. He reached for the sky as if being caught red-handed during a bank robbery.

"Touchdown Titans!" the announcer howled.

Lone Tree's head coach bull-rushed the head official while his assistant coaches ushered their players back to the locker room. The ceremonial postgame handshake would have to wait until basketball season. Fans stormed out of the bleachers to celebrate the district win with their Boys of Fall. Coach War soaked in the moment. Members of the student body, teachers, staff, parents, and community patrons congregated around the Titans' logo at the fifty-yard line. They looked on as players took a knee around Coach War. When it was quiet, he yelled out.

"IT'S A GREAT DAY FOR FOOTBALL!"

The group cheered.

"Now that was game day grit!"

More cheering.

"No one told you it would be easy, but you found a way to get the job done!"

The players whooped, patting each other on the back.

"This one is special," he stated, thinking about President Kennedy. "Not because it was easy, but because it was hard."

Again the players cheered.

"Enjoy this, but don't be satisfied. It's a nice team win, but it's not our goal. We have more to climb, but the summit is in sight. We will acclimate to our new surroundings, then try to ascend to another base camp next week. If we are going to meet our goals, we cannot lose sight of what's in front of us. Stay away from the rat poison! Coaches, anything to add?"

One by one the eight assistant coaches shared how proud they were of the players' attitude, effort, grit, and resilience. Coach War stepped out of the semi-circle to observe the scene. He truly loved this team. In the locker room, "Hey Ya" by OutKast blasted from the speakers. Coach War did a brief dance solo before mingling amongst his athletes. He walked down the line, stopping at each locker to shake hands with every Titan, thanking them for their contribution to the team effort. He savored every second, wishing that the night and this feeling would not end.

* * *

It was after midnight when Coach War finally got home. He entered through the garage, removing his shoes in the darkness before slowly turning the doorknob to enter the house. He moved like a ninja, knowing that he'd catch hell from his wife if he woke up the kids. Standing in a dark laundry room, he slipped out of his khakis and polo, trading it for gray sweat pants and his favorite Cubs T-shirt. He embraced the familiar feel of the shirt's polyester-cotton blend. For the first time all day, he allowed himself to relax and smile. His cell phone buzzed against the stainless steel of the washing machine with a Twitter notification from Remmy. Coach War made his way down the hall to the master bedroom. He slithered under the covers next to

Laura in their king-size bed. A huge grin covered his face as he viewed the message from one of his most valued True Titans.

"Big 'W' tonight—thanks for trusting me at the end."

Setting his phone on the floor beside the bed, Coach War closed his eyes and fell asleep. His heart was full.

Chapter Fifty-Three

The Phone Call

A loud ringtone interrupted the quiet darkness of the master bedroom. Coach War jolted upright, bending at the waist, his torso rising out of the covers. He rubbed his eyes, shielding them from the blinding strobe light that was lighting up the room from the back of his phone. Coach War glanced at the clock on top of Laura's dresser next to the bed. It was 2:33 a.m. *Someone had better have died.* Laura shushed the baby back to sleep, then took out her frustration on her husband.

"Who is that!" she demanded, covering their son's ears with her hands. She pressed him into her chest to feed and sooth him, before sinking back under the covers.

"Bill Allen," Coach War responded, looking at the phone's caller ID. "He wouldn't drunk dial me, would he?" His finger glided across the bottom of the screen to answer the call.

"Hello?"

"Coach," Mr. Allen said, his voice slow and deliberate, "sorry to bother you so late. I must've woke up your entire household." Mr. Allen sniffled.

"I think he's been crying," Coach War said to Laura, muffling his phone's receiver with his left hand.

"It's fine," Coach War assured him. "What's going on?"

"Mit… Mitch… Mitchell…" Mr. Allen stammered, unable to bring himself to say his name.

"Yes, Mitchell?" Coach questioned, swinging his legs over the edge of the bed. "Did something happen?"

"Mitchell's gone."

"Gone? Like missing?" Coach War asked.

"Gone like *dead*," Mr. Allen clarified, bursting into a loud sob. The words pierced Coach War's heart like a knife.

"Oh, wow," Coach War whispered, tipping his head back as he covered his mouth with his free hand.

There was a long silence on the phone.

"I'm sorry," Mr. Allen said, regaining his composure. "You had a big win tonight, and I don't want to be a Debbie Downer, but I thought you should be one of the first to know. I'm just not really able to talk right now. Can we meet tomorrow?"

"Yeah. I'll be at school in the morning to upload film."

"Not at school. How about ChapaChino? Ten a.m.?"

"Works for me," Coach War confirmed.

"Good, we can talk more then."

Mr. Allen blew his nose directly into the speaker. Coach War cringed, lifting the phone away from his ear.

"Bill," Coach War said, with the wonder of a small child, his tone meek. "I'm so sorry. Thanks for letting me know."

Coach War pressed the red icon on his touch screen, ending the call.

"Everything OK?" Laura asked, barely half-awake.

"No," Coach War responded, lying back down. "Mitchell is dead."

He rolled over, wrapping his arms around his wife and infant son. When he closed his eyes, tiny beads of moisture fell softly onto Laura's skin.

Chapter Fifty-Four

Weddings Are Optional

Dark red rims circled Mr. Allen's eyes the next morning. He spotted Coach War sipping his coffee at a booth in the back corner. Mr. Allen shuffled past the other patrons and waiters, making his way to join Coach War.

"You look terrible," Coach War initiated, extending a tall cardboard cup toward Mr. Allen. "Here, this might help. It's Mitchell's favorite cappuccino."

"Thanks." Mr. Allen squeezed the cup. He liked how the hot coffee burnt against the skin of his hand as it radiated from the to-go cup. "If only this sting could replace the pain of losing Mitchell."

"How are you holding up?" Coach War asked, concerned for his friend's emotional state.

"I'll get through it." Mr. Allen said, wiping his nose with a napkin. "Mitchell was my high school English teacher and football coach. I've always looked up to Coach McClellen. He was there for me when nobody else was. I didn't have a dad in my life, so I guess Coach just kind of filled that void." He paused for a moment. "Actually, *he's* the reason *I* became a teacher and a coach." Fresh tears pooled in Mr. Allen's eyes.

"How'd he pass?"

Mr. Allen took a second to gather himself, drying his eyes with the same napkin.

"Lung cancer. He's been battling it for a few years now, but he's kept that part of his life very private out of respect for his family."

"So *that's* why that nagging cough was uncontrollable at times," Coach War said, leaning away from the table and into the booth. "Have you heard anything about when the arrangements might be?"

"The family is still working out the details, but it sounds like Tuesday."

Of course the funeral would be Tuesday, Coach War thought, grinning at the irony. *That's what Mitchell would've wanted.* Coach War let Mitchell's sing-songy voice play in his head… "We are Tuesday people."

"Are you going to take a personal day?" Mr. Allen asked rhetorically.

Coach War shrugged his shoulders, lifting the cardboard cup to his lips.

"I'm not sure. Who will run practice? We're in the middle of a championship run, and I don't want there to be any distractions as we continue to climb Mount Everest."

"You're going to miss Mitchell's funeral because of *practice?*" Mr. Allen questioned. "Practice can wait! You only get one chance to say goodbye. After all he's done for you, sharing some of the precious time he had remaining with you, you're really *not* going to go say goodbye?"

A long moment of tension passed, allowing Mr. Allen to gather himself.

"Look," he said, lowering his voice, "you are a better coach today having had the opportunity to meet with Mitchell, correct?"

"Absolutely," Coach War confirmed.

"And your program's culture is better because of the work you two have done?"

Coach War looked down at his right wrist. He nervously twisted the team wristband until the theme "Sharpen the Axe" was centered across the bone of his arm. He stared at the phrase, thinking about the lumberjack.

"There's no doubt that my axe is sharper from having known Mitchell."

"Well, then you should know what the right thing to do is. Coach McClellen used to share a lot of those same things with us in high school. He couldn't rely on who would be in our life outside of our huddle, or what advice we would receive, so he used his platform as a coach to impart some of his wisdom to us. He encouraged us to give up the ways of being a boy and grow into becoming a man."

Coach War was all ears. He shifted forward in his seat, resting his elbows on the table.

"He used to talk in this thick Italian accent…" Mr. Allen laughed as tears fell like cinder blocks down his cheeks. "I mean like he was just off the boat from Italy."

Mr. Allen's belly shook with each sob.

"He would joke that he was 'cooking spaghetti, ah!'" Mr. Allen made a triangle, pinching his pointer finger, middle finger, and thumb together, raising them to his lip. He released his hand into the air the way a satisfied chef might after perfecting a signature dish.

Mr. Allen continued in the terrible Italian accent.

"I-ma throwin' spaghetti against the wall and-a hopin' somethin' sticks."

Coach War laughed as Mr. Allen sipped his morning brew. "Total Dad move."

"I know, terrible, right?" Mr. Allen agreed. "Anyway, one of the things that has stuck with me is how a *man* handles major life events." He let his mind revert back to his fifteen-year-old self, when he was a sophomore and Mitchell was his coach.

* * *

Billy Allen grabbed at the cool, green grass, enclosing a tuft of the turf in his fist. He twisted the blades, ripping them from the earth, only to watch them dance in mid-air as they fell back to the dirt. Leaning hard against his helmet, he mustered all of his remaining energy in an attempt to stay upright. Billy clenched his eyelids, preventing the sweat rolling down his forehead from stinging his eyes. Coach McClellen was standing amid a semicircle of players, and Billy did his best to listen to his transformational coach, despite the temporary discomfort.

Mr. Allen recalled the younger version of Mitchell as if the memory had happened yesterday. A green flat-bill hat rose off his forehead like a skyscraper. His trademark white, pocketed T-shirt was neatly tucked into gray Bike coaching shorts, the top two buttons clasped together at the belly button. White, knee-high tube socks with two green rings completed the look. Coach McClellen's whistle hung around his neck, dangling in the late summer breeze.

* * *

Mr. Allen spoke to Coach War in a gravelly voice, doing his second impression of the old ball coach.

"'Men,' he would say, 'in life you will be confronted with two events—weddings and funerals. People get married and people die. Here's my advice... weddings are optional, but funerals, funerals are mandatory.'"

"Why?" Coach War asked, bringing Mr. Allen back to the present.

"Well," Mr. Allen explained, "weddings are joyous times, even ones you may not *want* to miss. But if you *can't* be there, you can reproduce that good time on another occasion."

Coach War nodded.

"Funerals are different because those events cannot be duplicated. Whenever you attend a funeral your behavior says 'this is a person who matters to me. They made a difference in my life. I *owe* it to them to be there.' Funerals are an important showing of a person's legacy."

"But we are in the middle of the season," Coach War complained, turning his attention back to the semantics of Mitchell's funeral. "What do I do about practice? I can't just *miss* school and practice. Mitchell would understand."

"But I thought you are a *Tuesday* person," Mr. Allen reminded him with just a hint of guilt.

Coach War hung his head.

"Of course I'm a *Tuesday* person," Coach War sighed, staring at the ground.

"Look," Mr. Allen continued. "It's your decision. You're an adult, and you can determine what the right thing to do is. But, don't you tell your team that at the end of the day they must look themselves in the mirror and feel good about the decisions they've made? Will *you* be able to pass the Mirror Test if you miss this chance to say goodbye?"

Coach War looked deep into his friend's eyes.

"All I'm asking, I guess, is can you *do* the things you *say* you stand for?"

Coach War's face reddened, showing his embarrassment. He was ashamed of his selfish behavior. *How could I have even* contemplated *missing Mitchell's funeral?* he reflected, rising out of the booth.

"Well," he concluded, "if funerals are mandatory, then I guess that settles it." He patted Mr. Allen on the shoulder. "See you Tuesday."

Mr. Allen stood up too. "I thought so." He winked, pulling Coach War in closer for a comforting hug.

Chapter Fifty-Five

Through the Window

Using a personal day was a small price to pay to honor Mitchell, Coach War's friend and mentor, and Coach Roman was more than qualified to run practice. Laura accompanied her husband to the funeral on Tuesday. While she had never met Mitchell, she had heard a lot about him and wanted to pay her respects for all of the time and energy he invested in her husband. The cabin of the car was silent for the nearly hour drive to Cedar Creek.

The Warringtons met up with the Allens in the parking lot, then they sat together toward the back of the church. The atmosphere was somber. Black suits and dark dresses dotted the solid oak pews that lined the sanctuary. There was standing room only by the time the preacher moved to the pulpit, his black robe swaying to the side with every step.

"It is with a heavy heart that we gather here today to honor the life of a great man," the preacher announced into the microphone. The church was silent.

"While we mourn the loss of Mitchell McClellen, let us rejoice in knowing his spirit will rest in heaven for eternity."

The preacher asked the crowd to bow their heads, then he lowered his, closing his eyes to recite a prayer that concluded with an "Amen," which the congregation repeated. He lifted his head to look out at the crowd and spoke in a low, breathy voice.

"The ancient Greeks believed that a society grows great when men grow old and plant trees whose shade they will never see. As a son, brother, husband, father, teacher, coach, and friend, Mitchell planted countless trees. Today those seeds, the fruits of his labor, sit in rows around you. *You* are the shade of *his* forest."

Laura weaved her arm inside Vinny's, resting her hand on top of his.

"We know that we cannot live here on earth forever," the preacher continued. "Let us learn from thc Greeks. While one tree may fall, the forest lives on."

In true Mitchell fashion, the message to the congregation was hopeful and uplifting. Coach War sat tall in the pew, struck by a new insight, connecting the eulogy to the lumberjack. *If the "forest" is a metaphor for the people around you, then every tree that is cut down represents the death of someone close to you. That would make the lumberjack God.* The wheels continued to turn in Coach War's mind. *That's it! The axe is our faith! The sharper the axe, the greater our faith. The greater our faith, the more people we can impact! The more people we impact, the larger the forest. The larger the forest, the greater our legacy!* He repeated the preacher's words in his mind. *"While one tree may fall, the forest lives on."*

A small choir began to sing "Our God is an Awesome God." Coach War leaned into his wife, whispering in her ear for a pen. She rolled her eyes, then released his hand to lift the purse to her lap. Trying to be discrete, Laura slowly unzipped her purse and rummaged around the bottom of the bag. She grasped a pen and passed it to her husband. In the margin of Mitchell's funeral program, he wrote down the eulogy's message and his conclusion about the forest and the lumberjack. When the song was over, the preacher reassumed his position behind the pulpit.

"I was blessed to have known Mitchell for many years. He was a true servant-leader, willing to do anything to help others succeed. Muhammad Ali believed that 'service to others is the rent you pay for your room here on earth.' Mitchell used to say that every great servant-leader needs two things… a mirror and a window."

Coach War had never heard Mitchell talk about a window. He listened to the familiar description about the importance of having a mirror, anxiously waiting to hear about the window.

"The second tool a servant-leader needs is a window. A window allows leaders to share credit with the people around them. Mitchell's window was always open. He understood that no one becomes successful by themselves, and he willingly shared the glory with anyone deserving of a thank you. Through his window, Mitchell showed humility and a connectedness to others. One of the reasons he was able to plant so many trees was because his biggest successes were shared experiences. He was the most grateful human that I have ever known. Mitchell McClellen was a transformational leader because he had the courage to look into a mirror when things were going wrong and the humility to share credit with others through his window."

The preacher shifted his message to the congregation.

"Let us all use these two tools to be like Mitchell. When shouldering blame and responsibility, have the courage to look in the mirror. When having success, share credit by recognizing the efforts of those around you."

The preacher paused. He took two steps back from the pulpit, bowing his head before mouthing the words "Thank you, Mitchell." When he leaned into the microphone again, he brought his message full circle.

"*You* are Mitchell's forest. While he is gone, *you* are still here. Take a moment and think about a time when you needed Mitchell."

The church was silent. Coach War reflected on their Tuesday meetings.

"Well, now Mitchell needs *you* to be a good ancestor. Stand tall, honor Mitchell's legacy, and keep his forest alive and growing."

The preacher moved away from the pulpit, taking a seat in a chair behind the wooden altar. As the choir sang "On Eagle's Wings," Mitchell's family stood up, moving out of their reserved pew to the side of his casket where they would greet the congregation of individuals. Laura put her right arm around her husband's waist, squeezing into him as they walked down the aisle toward the casket.

* * *

On the drive home, Laura stared at her husband, who used his left hand to steer while she held his right hand between both of hers.

"Do you have any regrets?" she asked, looking at the curvature of his face. "His death was so sudden. Did you ever tell him thank you for everything he did to help you grow into a better leader?"

"No, I never got the chance to thank him because our work wasn't finished. He only told me about the first two phases in The Process of the 'Ship. I don't know what the last phase is! I know that it's selfish, but I don't understand why he had to die! Not yet anyway. I know that I should be more grateful, but now I'll never know what I need to do to elevate the performance of my team. It's not fair!"

Laura looked at her husband, giving him a taste of his own medicine.

"Stop pouting," she scolded. "Control what you can control, and ask yourself… what would Mitchell tell you? You've spent enough time with him. What would he suggest you do?"

Coach War focused on the road. The yellow lines that divided the highway brushed away in a blur, just like Coach War's time with Mitchell.

"Something tells me that God has a plan," she resumed, this time in a softer, more comforting voice, "and Mitchell's death is part of it. It's like the preacher was saying… you are part of his forest, so he lives on. Keep working on the things Mitchell told you to, and the final phase in this process-thingy will be revealed to you in due time."

"Not this time," Coach War said, shaking his head. "It's too late, I don't know what to do."

The Warringtons drove the rest of the way home in the quiet comfort of their SUV.

Chapter Fifty-Six

The Summit

The Titans went 1-0 in weeks six, seven, eight, and nine. The players had become a tight-knit group; they truly were a team. Every Thursday the players looked forward to Titan Talk. The True Titans continued to meet on a regular basis and were the team's catalysts, not Coach War and his coaching staff. They used the "Titan Tough" MVP daily to hold their teammates accountable. As a result of these efforts, the Titans had climbed the mountain together in small increments, establishing base camps along the way to acclimate to their surroundings. The team's mission to be 1-0 each week helped individuals stay away from the rat poison.

The Titans danced after every win, sharing success with each other and affirming the team culture Coach War had worked so hard to create. On the bus ride home after winning their final regular season game, the players talked, enjoying each other's company. Coach War sat alone in the front seat. He reflected on his team's progress, smiling when he heard Coach Heartwell's familiar voice play inside his mind.

"*You're going in this direction, or you're going in this direction... this is a lie.*"

There was no steeper trend line than the one the Titans were on.

As the wheels of the team's varsity bus rolled down the highway, with the JV and freshmen buses in tow, Coach War thought of Mitchell. Sitting next to him in the vacant green canvas seat was the prize they had worked so hard to earn… a large, three-foot by five-foot white banner. Written in red letters above the state's athletic association logo was "Football," followed by "District Champions" written below. Coach War stared at the coveted banner in the dim bus light.

"Championships!" Coach War exclaimed out loud. "That's it!"

It was an *aha* moment.

"Relationships and player leadership manifest into championships. This is The Process of the 'Ship." *I get it now! Thank you, Mitchell!*

Coach War closed his eyes; he summoned the lumberjack and smiled. The Titans were back in the playoffs.

* * *

On "Mirror Test Monday," Coach War rolled the tape, emphasizing the same message that helped his team reach the summit of Mount Everest.

"Be 1-0," he told his Titans, reminding them that the postseason was single-elimination. "Win, and we move on. Lose, and your season ends just like that." Coach War snapped his fingers.

On Tuesday, the Titans packed their own parachute, implementing the game plan, and by Wednesday, they all believed that they would be successful on game day. They fully trusted Coach War and his staff, and the True Titans led another installment of Titan Trust. The topic of conversation that night at dinner was: "What have you done to help the team sharpen its axe throughout the season?" After everyone had shared in their table groups, Coach War spoke to his team.

"Lumberjacks," he announced, speaking from the heart, "your axe is sharp. There is nothing else you can do to be ready for tomorrow night. It's time to go to work. Let's go chop some trees!"

Friday began with an epic morning pep rally. It seemed like the whole town had crammed into the gym to show their support for the Titans. That night in the locker room before kickoff, Coach War's final message to his team was about the Titan Football legacy, which was also part of Mitchell's forest now. Ten minutes before hitting the field for pregame warm-ups, the players huddled around Coach War. He stared at his assistant coaches, who were standing shoulder to shoulder behind the players.

"Coaches," Coach War asked, pointing down the line, "what number did you wear in high school?"

"Fifty-two," Coach Roman shouted.

"Seven," replied Coach Hogan.

The other coaches shared too.

"What was your number, Coach?" Remmy asked.

"Twenty-seven, in honor of the Broncos great safety Steve Atwater. See, your jersey is your legacy. Your number stays with you. It's your job as a member of this community to leave your jersey in a better place than when you got it. When you come back, in ten or twenty years, you'll sit in the stands and *wish* you were in our huddle for one more night. You'll watch the game with your wife, your kids, or maybe even an old teammate, and you'll scan the sideline, searching for your number. When you spot it, you'll look at the kid, sizing him up. You won't care if he is the team captain or makes the game-winning catch, you just want to see that someone has your number and that they give great effort when your number is called."

Coach War paused to take a sip from his Gatorade bottle, then continued, lowering his voice.

"Gentlemen, your jersey is not *your* jersey, it's rented. It belongs to something bigger than yourself. At the end of the season, your jersey will go back into the closet for the rest of the year. Some of you will be reissued that same jersey next year. Others of you will leave it behind for another Titan to wear. Before your season is over, make sure your jersey is in a better place than when you got it. Make sure your jersey has lots of stories to tell. Let's make some memories tonight. I'm proud of this team, and I love you. True Titans, you got 'em."

Coach War faded into the shadows of the locker room. The True Titans stood up, taking center stage. This was their team, and it was now their opportunity to motivate each other. Coach War totally trusted his leadership council. The soles of his Nike Free shoes squeaked against the cement as he exited the locker room. He pushed the heavy steel door open, beginning a solitary walk toward the field. Tonight, Coach War was the lumberjack, and he was carrying a razor-sharp axe. He walked along the sidewalk, passing through the hurricane fence gate and onto the track. The Titan band spotted Coach War enter the stadium and broke into "All I Do Is Win." At the conclusion of the song, a drumline roll-off led into the school song. Coach War turned back to look for his team; they were right behind him. He nodded to his players, then ran onto the turf, excited for another day of work in the forest.

Notes and Dedications

This book is a testament to the individuals who have made a deep impact on my life. The chapters and events throughout the story are a compilation of shared experiences.

Chapter Six is dedicated to Troy Jepsen. Troy is a transformational leader and was my direct supervisor at Iowa State University. I appreciate your zest for life and sports, and highly prize the hours we spent together in the equipment room. Your advice, perspective, and winning attitude continue to influence me beyond the Bergstrom Football Complex. Thank you, Troy, for leading with character and being a mentor for every member of Team Troy!

Chapter Fourteen is dedicated to Shari Warner. Mrs. Warner was at the end of her distinguished teaching career when I was beginning mine. Mrs. Warner's philosophy of "Pack Your Own Parachute" has become my personal mantra on the importance of preparedness and is a message I continue to share with the athletes I coach. Thank you, Mrs. Warner, for believing in me and for being an outstanding model for a young teacher to follow.

Chapter Fourteen is also dedicated to Brian Knott. Coach Knott gave me my first job in high school athletics, modeling for me the principles that come with the title of coach and leader. The time I spent on his staff, along with our deep playoff runs, are memories that I will always cherish. Thank you, Coach Knott, for showing me how to create a legacy that is built on more than just winning.

Chapter Fifteen is dedicated to Larry Goodrich, my 7th grade football coach. Coach Goodrich is one of the most enthusiastic people

I know. Every day, rain or shine, at the end of calisthenics, Coach Goodrich would start practice by yelling, "IT'S A GREAT DAY FOR FOOTBALL!" Thanks, Coach Goodrich, for being the first transformational leader in my life and modeling the energy that every great leader should impart to their teams. Nearly thirty years later, I can still hear your voice filled with positive energy, and it's always a great day for football!

Chapter Sixteen is dedicated to Chuck Earleywine. No matter the weather, you could count on Coach Earleywine to be wearing shorts. In the event of a blizzard, he might wear snow boots too, but that was a rare occasion. Coach Earleywine always kept our team focused on the task, not the weather. While Coach Earleywine is no longer with us, his legacy lives on today. Thanks, Chuck, for showing me how to capture the hearts of my athletes.

Chapter Twenty-Two is dedicated to Bill Lafleur. Aside from being a dynamic professional, Bill's integrity and high character make him a valuable leader. Thanks, Bill, for always being willing to share an administrator's perspective on the issues we face in education today.

Chapter Twenty-Three is dedicated to Fran Schwenk, my transformational college football coach. Inappropriate language was not tolerated within his program and the "firetruck" cliché is one of the principles he used to transform boys into men. Chapter Thirty-Seven is also dedicated to Coach Schwenk. I still treasure many of his handwritten notes and their familiar words, written in all caps, that always bring a smile to my face. Thank you, Coach Schwenk, for your patience and character, and for helping me evolve from a boy into the man I am today.

Chapters Twenty-Five and Fifty-Four are dedicated in loving memory of Daryl Bunch. Daryl was an influential leader who invested time, energy, and money in others, reveling in their individual growth and success. Thank you, Daryl, for seeing my potential at an early age and sharing your secrets of success as I grew into a young professional. Daryl really enjoyed combining business and pleasure, and I value the memories we made together.

Chapter Twenty-Six is dedicated to Randy Jackson. Few leaders invest the time and energy to build a transformational culture like Coach Jackson. He is accessible, passionate, and always looking to improve his team's chemistry. His book *Culture Defeats Strategy* is a MUST-READ for any leader. His experience and ideas have revolutionized our high school football program.

Chapter Thirty is dedicated to Doane Football. Doane University is a special place, but few places on campus are as dear to me as Simon Field, the one-hundred-yard classroom. The experiences and traditions of our historic football program reach far beyond wins and losses. My legacy is tied to this elite band of brothers. "Merrill Will Ring!"

Chapter Thirty-Three is dedicated to Chad Van Kley. This story would not be possible without your effort and commitment to serving others. Thank you for making the culture of Monarch Football a top priority. Also, thank you for giving me a platform to serve others by "believing in something bigger than myself." I value your friendship and support and enjoy doing the "dirty work" with you and our coaching staff as we work to accomplish shared goals.

Chapters Thirty-Four and Fifty are dedicated to Craig Bogatzke. Your concept of dividing time and energy equally among students has heightened my awareness of how I distribute these resources on a daily basis. You are one of my favorite people to be around, and I appreciate our conversations on sports and life. Thank you, Coach Bogatzke, for helping me keep home plate the standard seventeen inches.

Chapter Thirty-Eight is dedicated to Logan Maxwell, a driven young professional and influential leader. I had the privilege of hosting Logan in my classroom as he completed his student teaching experience. During our time together, I am sure that I learned more from Logan than he did from me. Logan not only writes notes to his athletes, but he also attaches a small monetary unit to the letter. Thanks, Logan, for helping me build my classroom's culture and influencing me to take my handwritten graduation letters to the next level.

Chapter Forty-Two is dedicated to Evan Wiebers. Evan is an irreplaceable member of the Monarch Football family and one of my biggest champions. As a three-year starter and two-time team MVP, Evan is a proven leader and producer, and I highly value our relationship, both on and off the field. Thanks, Evan, for always believing in me and encouraging me. I look forward to continuing our relationship for many years to come. Go chase your dreams!

Chapter Forty-Five is dedicated to the Alpha Omega fraternity at Doane University. Thank you to my brothers for helping me transition from an awkward teenager into a man. The lessons I learned as an active continue to shape the decisions I make as an adult. Thank you for endless stories, fellowship, and allowing me to be part of a great legacy.

Chapter Fifty-One is dedicated to Adam Burns. Coaches' get-togethers and outings, post-practice discussions in the locker room, long bus rides, and JV football games would not be the same without you. You are a passionate leader. I appreciate serving our team with you and value your friendship.

Chapter Fifty-Two is dedicated to Charlie Wiebers. In addition to being one of my favorite students of all-time in the classroom, Charlie is passionate about athletics. You are a cerebral young player and always bring the sauce to the huddle. I can't wait to see what you will accomplish as you finish high school and become an adult. The sky's the limit!

Additional Acknowledgments

First and foremost, thank you to my family, specifically to my wife Rachel. Thank you for tolerating the infinite hours I spend away from our young family pursuing my dreams. I could not passionately teach and coach without your unconditional support and love. Thanks for being the rock of our family. And to my kids, Scarlet, Aven, and Maddux… thanks for motivating me to be a better person every day. You keep my axe sharp and are my biggest contribution to the future and my greatest legacy.

A special thanks to my mom and dad, Suzanne and Marty Torrey. You have instilled in me the value of being a life-long learner. Thank you for the unconditional love and support as I continue to chase my dreams. You are my biggest champions and encouragers. Thank you for always being there for me and giving me the latitude to pursue worthy goals.

Thank you to my publisher and editors Ian Leask and Rick Polad for believing in me and helping this story evolve into a finished product. Also, a special thanks goes out to Kathy Campbell, who has been there from the very beginning. This project would never have materialized without your guidance and encouragement. And to Donna Wilson, who is always willing to lend an ear and take a look.

Andy Bunch has always been a close personal friend. In Kindergarten, Andy identified me as his best friend. Over thirty years later, Andy's friendship and support remain invaluable. Our conversations, usually centered on sports and business, energize me and remind me of my purpose, just as iron sharpens iron. Thanks, Andy, for being there from the beginning. You are the bridge that links my past to the future.

To my colleagues, specifically Ryan Marzen, Tom Lipovac, Louis Cicenia, Mike Pardun, Patricia Ryan, Adam Mich, Jacob Brawner, Nick Potts, and Brian Slater, the staff at Denison Middle School, and all Monarch Coaches… thank you for believing in me as a teacher-leader and writer and investing precious time and energy into my work. I love serving in the trenches with you every day. The work we do together changes the world.

To my past, present, and future athletes… Thank you for giving my life and work purpose. Many of the lessons sprinkled throughout this book are the result of our time together. I am grateful for countless hours we've shared in the classroom, weight room, library, on the practice field, in the locker room, on long bus rides, and under the Friday night lights. Thank you for committing to something bigger than yourself. You put yourself in the arena while others criticize our efforts from the stands. I value our relationships and the authentic memories we create together. My success as a teacher and coach will be visible through what author Joe Ehrmann calls the "Twenty Year Window." In twenty years, when former students and players come back and reconnect with me and are committed husbands, partners, fathers, friends, and leaders, then I will know that I have fulfilled my purpose as a coach. So, what kind of success will we have next season? I'll let you know in twenty years.

About the Author

John Torrey is a teacher and coach with over a decade of experience in the classroom and on the sidelines. As an equipment manager at Doane University in Crete, Nebraska, John interned with the University of Nebraska-Lincoln, worked three Super Bowls for the NFL, and, after graduating, held positions with Iowa State University Football and the San Francisco 49ers. In 2016, he earned a masters degree in coaching and athletic administration from Concordia University Irvine, where The Process of the 'Ship was created. Today John and his wife Rachel raise three children in Denison, Iowa, where he teaches Seventh Grade Social Studies and coaches high school football and wrestling.

Connect with Coach Torrey on Twitter: @JTorreyAuthor.